Elisha Hoffman

Spiritual songs No. 2

For gospel meetings and the Sunday school

Elisha Hoffman

Spiritual songs No. 2
For gospel meetings and the Sunday school

ISBN/EAN: 9783337266370

Printed in Europe, USA, Canada, Australia, Japan

Cover: Foto ©Thomas Meinert / pixelio.de

More available books at **www.hansebooks.com**

SPIRITUAL SONGS

No. 2,

FOR

GOSPEL MEETINGS

AND THE

SUNDAY SCHOOL,

— BY —

REV. ELISHA A. HOFFMAN,

AND

J. H. TENNEY.

PUBLISHED BY

SAMUEL BARKER,

No. 74 Superior St., Cleveland, O.

SPIRITUAL SONGS NO. 2.

The Quiet Vale Of Prayer.

MARIA WHEELER.   E. A. HOFFMAN.

Expressivo.

1. O qui - et vale of pray'r, sweet pray'r, The fragrance of God's
2. Lone wea - ry hearts oppressed with grief, Can wan - der there and
3. O qui - et vale of pray'r, I've found A treas - ure on thy
4. And though my fal - t'ring feet may stray From truth, to er - ror's

peace is there; Its ho - ly paths, o'er shin - ing sod, Are
find re - lief, Or, for the toil of life prepare, With-
hal - lowed ground; The pre - cious seal of trust - ing love In
trou - bled way, For - giv - ing love will meet me there, With-

wa - tered by the hand of God.
in that sa - cred vale of pray'r.
God, who rules the spheres a - bove.
in that quiet vale of pray'r.

Refrain

O qui - et

pp Ritard.

vale, sweet vale of pray'r! The fragrance of God's peace is there.

JESUS IS CALLING EOR THEE.

GRACE GLENN.

J. H. FILLMORE. by per.

3

1. When, as of old, in her sad-ness   Ma ry sat weep-ing a - lone,
2. Oh, when thy pleasures are flow-ing,   Fad-ing thy hope and thy trust,
3. Down by the shore of death's riv-er,   Some-time thy footsteps shall stray,

Soft - ly the voice of her ,sis - ter   Whispered, "The Master has come."
When of the dear-est earth-treasures   Dust shall re-turn un - to dust.
Where waits a boat-man to bear thee   O - ver to in - fi - nite day.

So in the depths of thy sor - row,   Gall tho' its foun-tain may be,
Then, tho' the world may in-vite thee,   Vain will its of - fer-ing be,
What then tho' dark be his shad-ow,   If when his com-ing thou see,

List, for there com-eth a whis-per,   Je-sus is call - ing for thee.
List, for there com-eth a whis-per,   Je-sus is call - ing for thee.
Cometh there soft - ly a whis-per,   Je-sus is call - ing for thee.

CHORUS.

Repeat pp

Call - ing, call - ing,   Jesus is calling for thee.
Call - ing for thee. call - ing for thee,

Sacred Season Of Communion.

E. A. HOFFMAN.   J. H. TENNEY.

1. 'Tis the hallowed hour of pray'r, And we trusting - ly bring All our
2. 'Tis the precious hour of pray'r, And we humbly en - treat: Fath - er,
3. 'Tis the sa - cred hour of pray'r, Calm as heav-en a - bove; Soul to

fears and doubtings there, Sin and want, ev - ery - thing; For we
breathe the Spir-it now As we bow at thy feet; Touch our
soul is breathing there The com-mun-ion of love; Ev - ery

know that God de - lights A glad welcome to give, And the
lips with pow'r of song: Fill our souls with thy love; And be-
heart is sweet - ly filled With a peace most profound; O the

Chorus.

blessings that we ask for We shall freely receive.
slow the benediction Of thy peace from above. Precious hour of pray'r, hallowed
place is like to Heaven Where such true joys abound!

Rit.

hour of pray'r, Sacred sea-son of com-mu-nion, It is sweet to be there!

The Child Of A King.

KATTIE BUELL. Alt.
DUET.

JOHN SUMNER, arr.

1. My fath - er is rich, not in hous - es and lands, But he
2. My fath - er's own son, the Sa - vior from sin, Once
3. I once was an out - cast, a stranger on earth, A
4. A tent or a cot - tage—O why should I care? They are

hold - eth the wealth of the world in his hands! The
wan - der'd o'er earth as the poor - est of men; But
sin - ner by choice, and an "a - lian" by birth; But
build - ing a pa - lace for me o' - ver there; Though

ru - bies and dia - monds, the sil - ver and gold Of the
now he is reign - ing for - ev - er on high, And will
I've been a - dopt - ed, my name's writ - ten down As an
ex - iled from home, yet still I may sing; All

Chorus

earth are all his; he has rich - es un - told.
give us a home in the sweet by and by. I'm the child of a King, The
heir to a mansion, a robe and a crown.
glo - ry to God, I'm the child of a King!

child of a King; With Jesus, my Sa - vior, I'm the child of a King.

Only Near To The Kingdom.

Mark. 12: 24.

Words and Music by W. JOHNSON.

1. To live in the land where the Christ pass - es by, To
2. To come to the Sa - vior with ques - tion and pray'r, His
3. Not far from the king - dom, yet not born a - gain; Not
4. Al - most in the king - dom, al - most to the gate That

go to the place where his Spir - it is nigh; To
an - swer of love and sal - va - tion to bear, To
far from the king - dom, yet cling - ing to sin; Not
stands o - pen wide in the way that is straight, Al -

know the sweet gos - pel of Je - sus the Lord, And
speak in his pres - ence ac - knowl - edge his word, And
far from the king - dom, close, close to the road, And
most, but not quite, O how fear - ful the word! Al -

Refrain

yet on - ly near to the kingdom of God.
yet on - ly near to the kingdom of God.
yet on - ly near to the kingdom of God.
most, yet but near to the kingdom of God.

Near to the kingdom,

Rit.

Near to the kingdom, And yet on - ly near to the kingdom of God.

Bringing In The Sheaves.

Matt. 13: 39.　　　　　　GEORGE A. MINOR.

1. Sowing in the morning, sowing seeds of kindness, Sowing in the noontide
2. Sowing in the sunshine, sowing in the shadows, Fearing neither clouds nor
3. Go, then, ever weeping, sowing for the Master, Tho' the loss sustain'd our

and the dew - y eve; Waiting for the harvest, and the time of reap - ing,
winter's chilling breeze; By and by the harvest and the la - bor end - ed,
spir - it oft-en grieves; When our weeping's o'er, He will bid us welcome,

Chorus.

We shall come, rejoicing, bringing in the sheaves.)
We shall come, rejoicing, bringing in the sheaves. }　(Bringing in the sheaves,
We shall come, rejoicing, bringing in the sheaves.)　)Bringing in the sheaves,

Bringing in the sheaves, We shall come, rejoicing, Bringing in the sheaves,　)
Bringing in the sheaves, We shall come, rejoicing, [OMIT. . Bringing in the sheaves,)

From "Golden Light."

Saved.

ABBIE MILLS.

E. A. HOFFMAN.

1. Je - ho - vah is my King, Low at his feet I
2. 'Twas he re - moved my guilt, I can - not tell you
3. From en - vy, and from pride, Which God can - not al-
4. To him who clean-seth me I will per - form my
5. Come, ev - 'ry wea - ry soul, Come, at his foot-stool

bow;.... With joy his wondrous love I sing, For
how;.... But this I know, his blood was spilt, And
low;.... From all his presence can - not bide, My
vow:.... His prais - es in my mouth shall be, For
bow; ... 'Tis Je - sus on - ly can make whole, And

Chorus.

Je - sus saves me now, The Lord re - moved my
Je - sus saves me now.
Je - sus saves me now.
Je - sus saves me now.

guilt...... I can - not tell you how;...... But

this I sure - ly know, That Je - sus saves me now.

Soldiers Of Zion.

Rev. R. Lowry. Rev. R. Lowry.

1. Soldiers of Zi - on, on we go, Brave are the hearts that face the foe,
Cho.—Soldiers of Zi - on, on we go, Brave are the hearts that face the foe,

Vic-t'ry awaits us, for we know, We fol-low the Lord our King;
Vic-t'ry awaits us, for we know, We fol-low the Lord our King;

Not by the might of hu-man arm, Not by the pow'r of each to harm,

But by the Spi-rit's ho - ly charm, Shall we the tri-umph sing.

2. Hark to the trump that sounds for war,
See how the flag goes on before,
Look how the ranks swell more and more
  As Jesus the King leads on:
Strong are the hosts of Sin and Death,
Stronger the might of Him who saith,
"I will consume them with my breath!"
  Then will the field be won. *Cho.*

3. Sure as the Truth, will dawn the day
When giant Wrong will end his sway,
Bondage and Error flee away,
  And earth to the Lord belong;
Courage, ye souls who fight and plod,
This is the path that worthies trod;
Gird up your loins, Elect of God;
  Soon comes the victor's song. *Cho.*

From "Our Glad Hosanna." by per. of Biglow & Main.

The Half Has Never Been Told.

FRANCES RIDLEY HAVERGAL. 1 Cor. 2: 9. R. E. HUDSON.

1. I know I love thee bet - ter, Lord, Than an - y earth - ly
2. I know that thou art near - er still Than an - y earth - ly
3. Thou hast put glad-ness in my heart; Then well may I be
4. O Sa - vior, pre-cious Sa - vior mine! What will thy presence

joy, For thou hast giv - en me the peace Which
throng And sweet - er is the thought of thee Than
glad! With - out the se - cret of thy love I
be If such a life of joy can crown Our

Chorus.

noth - ing can des - troy.
an - y love - ly song. The half has nev - er yet been
could not but be sad.
walk on earth with thee?

told, Of love so full and free; The half has nev - er yet been
yet been told,

Rit.

told, The blood— it cleanseth me.
yet been told, cleanseth me.

Why Not Trust In Him Now?

Mrs. E. W. Chapman.　　　　　　　　J. H. Tenney.

1. The Savior hath called thee and shown thee his love; He died for poor sinners like
2. His blood he hath shed to redeem thee from sin; A fount has been opened for
3. He'll clothe thee with vesture that's whiter than snow; In pastures of verdure will

thee; He left his bright home in the mansions a-bove, The
thee; He tells thee of heav-en, and bids thee come in, The
lead, Where wa-ters of life in a-bun-dance do flow, Thy

Chorus.

cap-tive from bond-age to free.
beauties of E-den to see. O, why not trust in him,
soul in its rap-ture to feed.

[trust in him] now? O, why not trust in him, [trust in him] now? He

loves thee, and bids thee on him to re-ly; O! why not trust in him now?

Make Me A Worker for Jesus.

E. E. REXFORD.　　　　　　　　　　　　　D. E. DORTCH, by per.

1. Make me a work-er for Je - sus, Steadfast, and earnest, and true,
2. Make me a work-er for Je - sus, Do-ing the task to be done.
3. Make me a work-er for Je - sus, Rea-dy to toil where he needs.
4. Make me a work-er, O Je - sus! Then at the set of the sun,

Will-ing to do for the Mas-ter All he expects me to do.
Cheerful-ly, earnest-ly, glad-ly Lab'ring till set of the sun.
Sow-ing good seed for the harvest, Plucking up bri-ars and weeds.
Say; Thou wert faithful, my servant, Rest, for thy work is now done.

Chorus.

Make me a work-er for Je - sus. Toil-ing faith-ful-ly,....

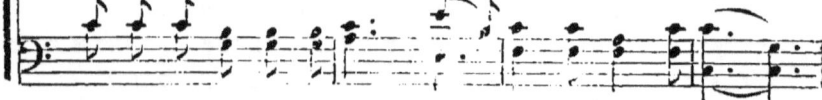

Do-ing my best for the Mas-ter; He has done great things for me.

Save The Boy!

"A foolish son is the heaviness of his mother."—Prov. 10: 1.

(TEMPERANCE SONG.)

Mrs. S. C. Ellsworth.   W. Warren Bentley, by per

SOLO.

[Life was dear to me;
1. Once he was so light and fair, Glad, and light and free, Fill'd my soul with peace and joy,
[stood, Till that dreadful hour.
2. Once he was so brave and true, Shunn'd the tempter's pow'r; Once for right he firmly
[Hold him to my side;
3. Once he was my only hope, Source of joy and pride, Then I thought that love might clasp,
[Looks with patient eye,
4. Tell him though he's wandered far, Love can never die, Lives in hope of his return,

[my darling boy.
But he took the fatal glass, 'Twas a fleeting joy. Drank, and lo, the hand of death, Grasp'd
[My poor wandering boy.
Bright and sparkling was the cup, Seem'd without alloy, Fair the hand that captive led,
[oh save my boy.
But today my boy forsakes Home with all its joy, Far in sin he's wandering now, Save,
[For the wandering boy.
Loving hearts have pleaded long, Pray'd for light and joy, Keeping still a welcome there

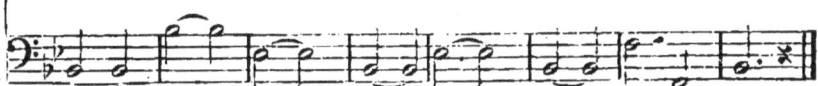

Chorus.

[Save, O save the boy.
Save the boy! Save the boy! Heav'n will ring with joy; Loving hearts are pleading now

14

In The Life-Boat.

Rev. WM. P. BREED, D. D. alt.   E. A. HOFFMAN.

1. Tossing on the bil-low, Rocking in the blast, Sick'ning on the pil-low,
2. Gone each earthly treasure, Cut away each mast, Vanished earthly pleasure.
3. Sorrows mul-ti-ply-ing, Prospects overcast, Weeping, groaning, sighing,

Verg-ing to the last; Skies all clad in sable, Storm clouds scudding past,
Still I'm anchored fast; For I rest in Je-sus, In whose arm of pow'r,
Still I'm anchored fast; Swiftly to my grave-bed, I am mak-ing haste,

Chorus.

Clinging to the ca - ble, I am anchored fast.
I'm se-cure-ly sheltered, Safe forevermore. I am in the Life-Boat,
Trembling 'neath the death-dread, Still I'm anchored fast.

I am in the Life-Boat, I am in the Life-Boat, Safe forevermore!

Standing On The Mighty Rock.

Psalms 40: 2.

A. W. FRENCH.   J. H. TENNEY.

1. Standing   on   the Migh - ty   Rock, Migh - ty   Rock, Migh-ty Rock,
2. Let the   wa - ters mad - ly sweep, mad - ly sweep, mad - ly sweep,
3. Some may   seek   the shift - ing   sand, Shift - ing   sand, shift-ing sand,
4. We have   suf - fered pain and   loss, Pain and   loss, pain and loss,

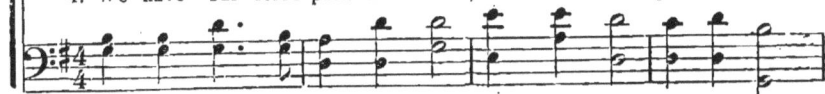

Far   a   bove   the bil - low's shock, Safe   with   Je - sus.
Care   we   not   if we may   keep   Close   to   Je - sus.
Ours   the bet - ter part to   stand, Safe   with   Je - sus.
Now   we   rest   be - neath the cross, Safe   with   Je - sus.

Chorus.

And   we cry: Christ is nigh;   {He   will guard our lit - tle flock,}
                                 {From the storm and bil - low's shock,}

Stand-ing   on   the Migh - ty   Rock, Safe   with   Je - sus.

Will You Be Washed In The Blood?

Words and Music by   Rev. 1: 5.   E. O. Excell, by per.

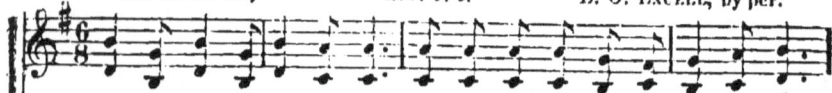

1. List, the Spir-it calls to thee, Will you be washed in the blood?......
2. Sinner, now this blessing claim; Will you be washed in the blood?......
3. Christ can wash you white as snow, Will you be washed in the blood?......
4. Je-sus drank the cup for all, Will you be washed in the blood?......

Je-sus died to make you free, Will you be washed in the blood?
Through the dear Redeemer's name, Will you be washed in the blood?
And the wit-ness you may know, Will you be washed in the blood?
Don't re-ject the Spir-it's call: Will you be washed in the blood?

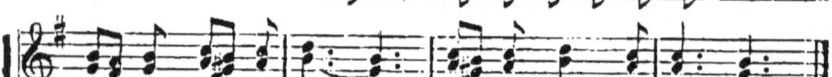

Par-don will be giv-en, Cleansing you for heav-en.
Claim him as your Sa-vior, He can save for-ev-er.
You can know this hour.... Of his sav-ing pow-er.
Grace is now a-bound-ing, Joy thro' heav'n resound-ing.

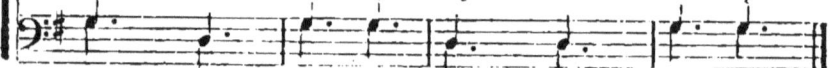

Chorus

Will you be washed, Washed in the blood of the Lamb?
Will you be washed in the blood of the Lamb?

Will you be washed, Washed in the blood of the Lamb?
Will you be washed in the blood of the Lamb?

Wonderful Love.

Words and Music by B. F. BLAKELY.

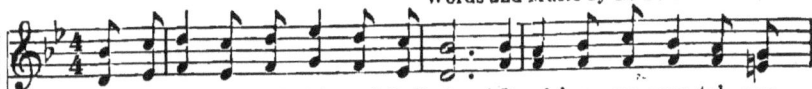

1. O the wonder-ful heights of God's love! Its riches no mor-tal can
2. When no arm could redeem fallen man, And hope had expired in each
3. O what glory there shines through his love On souls humbled low at his
4. I now walk in the sun-light of God; He washed and redeemed even
5. Light and glory are fill-ing my soul, My heart is o'erwhelmed with his

know; It has reached to the depths from a - bove To
breast, The Re - deem - er for sin - ners was slain; In
feet! They have hope of a man - sion a - bove; Their
me; I am saved, and the sin - cleans - ing blood My
love; 'Tis a well spring-ing up as a pool; The

Chorus.

an-som poor sin-ners from woe.
him they have pardon and rest.
peace and their joy is complete.   O the won-der-ful love, Of the
hope and re - joic-ing shall be.
fountain is Je - sus a - bove.

Fath - er a-bove, Who has washed and redeemed even me! With my

life's latest breath, And in Heav'n after death, This my song of rejoicing shall be.

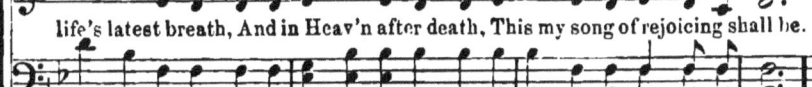

The Very Best for Jesus.

E. A. HOFFMAN.   J. H. LESLIE.

1. Give to Christ your best af-fec-tion! He is worthy to re - ceive,
2. Give your choicest hours to Jesus, In de-vo-tion pure and blest,

Love the purest and the warmest, All your trusting heart can give.
Hours most rich in tho't and feeling—He deserves the very best.

Chorus.

Give the ver - y best to Je - sus, Give to him the ver - y best.

In the giving, In the giv - ing You will be su-preme-ly blest.

3. Give to Christ your noblest talents!
   Use them in his sweet employ;
   In the using you will harvest
   A reward of blissful joy.—Ref.

4. Give your influence to the Savior!
   Bring no stain upon his name
   By a heart untrue and faithless,
   By a life of sin and shame.—Ref.

5. Give your soul, your all to Jesus,
   As a willing sacrifice;
   Your reward shall be a mansion
   In the shining Paradise.—Refrain.

From "Songs of Faith."

Have More Faith In Jesus.

Words and Music by E. A. HOFFMAN.

1. Full and perfect faith in Jesus,   O how wondrous is its pow'r!
2. Faith subdues the earth-ly kingdoms   In these hearts of sense and sin,
3. Faith removes the many mountains   Of our fear and un-be-lief,
4. Faith lays hold on God's strong promise, Touches Christ, the Father's Son,
5. Faith can stop the mouth of li-ons,   Quench the vi-o-lence of fire,
6. O for more such faith in Jesus,   Migh-ty faith in Christ, the Lord,
7. Have you such a faith, my brother?   Do you trust with all your heart?

Such a faith can save and keep us   Ev-'ry moment, ev-'ry hour.
Cleanses us from all de-file-ment   Brings the heavenly Kingdom in.
And un-seals the liv-ing fountains   Of God's grace for our re-lief.
Then the bless-ed Ho-ly Spi-rit   Brings the heavenly blessing down.
Make us strong to work or suf-fer,   And our hearts with zeal inspire.
Faith that holds God to his prom-ise,   To his sure, un-fail-ing word!
Seek it then, the Lord will give it   E'er from hence you shall depart.

Chorus.

Have more faith in Christ, my brother, Have more faith in Christ, your Lord;

In his faith-ful-ness con-fid-ing, Rest on his un-fail-ing word.

In The Shadow Of The Rock.

Ray Palmer.   A. J. Showalter. by per.

1. In the shad-ow of the rock let me rest, (let me rest,)
2. I in peace will rest me there till I see, (till I see,)
3. Then my pil-grim staff I'll take and once more, (and once more,)

When I feel the temp-est shock thrill my breast, (thrill my breast,)
That the skies a-gain are fair o-ver me, (o-ver me,)
I'll my on-ward jour-ney make as be-fore, (as be-fore,)

All in vain the storm shall sweep while I hide, (while I hide,)
That the burn-ing heats are past, and the day, (and the day,)
And with joy-ous heart and strong I will raise, (I will raise,)

Chorus.

And my tranquil sta-tion keep by Thy side.
Bids the tra-ve-ler at last go his way,   Then let me rest, oh,
Un-to Thee, O Rock, a song glad with praise.

Then let me rest, In the shadow of the Rock, let me rest, (let me rest.)

Then let me rest, oh, Then let me rest, In the shadow of the rock let me rest.

Calvary.

J. H. TENNEY.

1. There is a dear and hallowed spot, Oft pre-sent to my eye;
2. Oh, what a scene was there displayed, Of love and a - go - ny,
3. When faint - ing un-der guilt's dread load, Unto the cross I'll fly,
4. When the dark scene of death, the last Momentous hour draws nigh,

Fine.

By saints it ne'er can be for-got; That place is Cal - va - ry.
When our Re-deem-er bow'd his head, And died on Cal - va - ry.
And trust the mer - it of that blood Which flow'd on Cal - va - ry.
Then, with my dy - ing eyes, I'll cast A look on Cal - va - ry.

Chorus.

D.S.

That place is Cal - va - ry, That place is Cal - va - ry,
And died on Cal - va - ry, And died on Cal - va - ry,
Which flowed on Cal - va - ry, Which flowed on Cal - va - ry,
A look on Cal - va - ry, A look on Cal - va - ry,

The Hand To Which I Cling.

MARY D. BRINE, alt.   JAMES McGRANAHAN.

1. There's not a moment of each day That I do not need to cling To the
2. I'm blind, too blind to choose my way Through this strange, bewildering land, So I
3. And though it be through storm or shine, I am told to fol-low on, Yet it

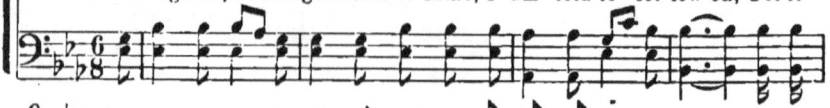

Migh-ty Hand which leadeth me, To the palace of my great King. My
dare not e'en for one brief moment, Let go of the Father's hand. And
matters not, since I may tread Where my Savior's dear feet have gone. And

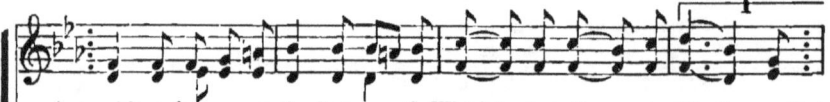

stumbling feet press the living path Which leads to the great white throne, But
well—ah! well do I know it, Lord— I ne'er can reach a - -
day and night as the moments pass, I may not see my guide, Yet
know, by faith in my trusting heart, That He is close at my - -
closer still to His hand I cling, By faith, by praise, and pray'r, Till
at His feet I shall lay me down, For - ev - er at rest from - -

Chorus.

lone.
side.   Then   to   his kind hand cling-ing,   I   dai-ly   fol-low,
care.

sing-ing, Because my soul he's bring-ing Up to the great white throne.

I Need Thee, Lord.

JOHN 15: 5. "Without me ye can do nothing."

E. A. HOFFMAN.　　　　　　　　CHAS. EDW. PRIOR, by per,

1. When cherished joys have tak - en wing, And sor - row wounds me
2. When sin has robbed me of my peace, And bro't me in - to

with its sting, Then to thy cross I fond - ly cling, For
sore dis-tress, And left me reft of hap - pi - ness, O

Refrain.

then I need thee Lord,
then I need thee Lord, I need thee, precious Lord! In thee my soul would hide! In

ev - 'ry time of need, Dear Christ, with me a - bide!

3. When at the cross, in anguish bent,
An humble, weeping penitent,
My tears and all my efforts spent,
O then I need thee, Lord!

4. When strong temptations come to me
To tear my trembling soul from Thee,
Then to thy cross for help I flee
For then I need thee, Lord.

5. When longs my soul for deeper rest,
To be with all thy fullness blest,
I lean me, then, upon thy breast,
For then I need thee, Lord,

6. I need thee, precious Lord, just now,
As at the mercy-seat I bow,
And offer up my solemn vow,
Just now I need thee, Lord.

The Golden Light.

Isa. 2: 5.

E. A. HOFFMAN.   GEORGE A. MINOR, by per.

1. Walk, my brother, in the light; Keep your soul-robes pure and white,
2. Walk - ing dai - ly in the light, All the way shall grow more bright;
3. Fol - low Je - sus in the light; Where he walks there is no night;
4. Walk in fel - low-ship of love Till you reach the home a - bove;

Spot-less, stain-less, free from sin, In the blood of Je - sus clean.
God his wealth of love will pour On your spir - it more and more.
All is per - fect, blissful day; Heaven's glo - ry floods the way.
They who fol - low in the light Shall with Je - sus walk in white.

Chorus.

Walk, walk in the light,.... Walk, walk in the light,....
Walk-ing in the golden light, We're walking in the golden light, We're

Repeat pp

Walk, walk in the light,. .. The golden light of God.
walk-ing in the golden light, The golden light of God.

Only In The Name Of Jesus.

25

"If ye shall ask anything in my name, I will do it."—JNO. 14: 14.

J. E. RANKIN, D.D   E. S. LORENZ.

1. There is peace on-ly in His name, On-ly in the name of Je - sus;
2. There is strength for the feeble heart, On-ly in the name of Je - sus;

And that peace, wretched souls may claim, Only in the name of Je - sus!
God will freely thus strength im-part, Claim it in the name of Je - sus!

Chorus.

Name of Je - sus, Name of Je - sus! When you pray, O pray in His

name! Go to God with ev - 'ry care; Tell it to Him in your pray'r,

On-ly in the name of Je - sus,

3. Tell to God, what your sins have been,
   Coming in the name of Jesus;
   He will make you all pure within,
   In the precious name of Jesus.

4. Tell to God what your weakness is,
   Tell it in the name of Jesus;
   Ask in faith, for to help is His,
   If you plead the name of Jesus.

From "Songs of Grace."

Satisfied By And By.

Theme of Chorus from Webster.
T. C. O'KANE, by per.

1. Enthroned is Je - sus now Up - on his heavenly seat; The
2. There we shall see his face, And nev-er, nev - er sin; There
3. Yes, and be-fore we rise To that im-mor - tal state The
4. Then let our songs a - bound, And ev-e ry tear be dry; We're

king - ly crown is on his brow, The saints are at his feet.
from the riv-ers of his grace, Drink endless pleasures in.
thoughts of such a-maz - ing bliss Should constant joys cre - ate.
marching, thro' Immanuel's ground, To fair - er worlds on high.

Chorus.

There with the glo.- ri-fied, Safe by our Sa-vior's side, We shall be

sat - is-fied By and by, By and by,

There, there with the glorified,

By and by, We shall be sat-is-fied By and by.

Safe, safe by our Savior's side.

Who Will Be There?

Mrs. E. C. Ellsworth.   J. H. Tenney.

1. Who will be one of the mul - ti-tude great, Sweeping with joy thro' the
2. Who will ascend with the Savior to be, Washed in the blood that is
3. Who will be sealed by the Lord as his own, Saved and re-joic - ing be-

bright pear-ly gate? Who of our number will still go a-stray,
flow - ing so free? Who will be rea - dy to en - ter the rest
fore the great throne? Who will be there to take part in the song,

Chorus.

Nev - er to en - ter the re - gions of day?
Christ has prepared in the home of the blest? Say, Oh, my brother,
Sung by the thousands who heavenward throng?

will you be there? Robes white and fair, Christ shall prepare

Rit. p

Tell me, my brother, will you be there? will you be there?

I've Found A Friend.

E. A. HOFFMAN.

1. I've found a friend, oh, such a friend! He loved me ere I knew him;
2. I've found a friend, oh, such a friend! He bled, he died to save me;
3. I've found a friend, oh, such a friend! All pow'r to him is giv-en;
4. I've found a friend, oh, such a friend! So kind, and true, and ten-der,

He drew me with the cords of love, And thus he bound me to him.
And not a-lone the gift of life, But his own self he gave me.
To guard me on my onward course, And bring me safe to heav-en.
So wise a coun-sel-lor and guide, So migh-ty a de-fend-er!

And 'round my heart still closely twine Those ties which naught can sever,
Naught that I have my own I call, I hold it for the giv-er;
The heaven-ly glories gleam a-far, To nerve my faint en-deav-or;
From him, who loves me now so well, What pow'r my soul can sev-er?

For I am his, and he is mine, For-ev-er and for-ev-er.
My heart, my strength, my life, my all, Are his, and his for-ev-er.
So now to watch, to work, to war, And then to rest for-ev-er.
Shall life and death, or earth or hell? No; I am his for-ev-er.

Rest, Sweet Rest.

W. B. TAPPAN.   IRA ORWIG HOFFMAN.

1. There is an hour of peace-ful rest, To mourning wanderers
2. There is a home for wea-ry souls, By sin and sor-row
3. There faith lifts up her cheer-ful eye To bright-er pros-pects
4. There fra-grant flow'rs immor-tal bloom, And joys supreme are

giv-en; There is a joy for souls distressed, A balm for ev-ery
driven,— When tossed on life's tempestuous shoals, Where storms arise and
giv-en And views the tempest pass-ing by, The evening sha-dows
giv-en; There rays di-vine disperse the gloom; Beyond the confines

Chorus.

wounded breast;'Tis found a-bove in heav-en.
o-cean rolls, And all is drear—but heav-en. There's sweet rest in
quick-ly fly, And all se-rene in heav-en.
of the tomb Appears the dawn of heav-en!

(in Heav'n.)

Heaven, There's sweet rest in Heav n, There's sweet rest in Heav'n, Sweet, sweet rest

Will You Come To The Cross?

To-day if ye will hear His voice, harden not your hearts.—Heb. 4: 7.

Mary E. Kail.   J. H. Leslie, by per.

Andante.

1. Sinner, come to the cross, For the moments are flying While around every
2. Will you come, sinner come, And accept of the glory? With thanksgiving and
3. Let the good news go home, That the lost are returning, While salvation's bright

where, Careless sinners are dying; Jesus calls you today, Will you gladly re-
[to de-
praise, Hear redemption's glad story; Learn the dear Savior's love, And His strength
lamp Is so brilliantly burning; Come to Jesus just now, With your burden of

Chorus.

ceive him? All he asks you to do, Is to trust and believe him.
liver, From the thraldom of sin, And to save you forever. Come to Jesus just
sorrow, For too late it may be, Should you wait for the morrow.

now, With your burden of sorrow, For too late it may be Should you wait for the morrow.

Waiting at the Cross.

"I waited patiently for the Lord; and he inclined unto me and heard my cry."—Psa, 40 : 4.

I. B.   I. BALTZELL, by per.

1   Sav - ior, at the cross I'm bend-ing,, All   to leave and follow thee;
2   All my talents, time, and treasure   I   surrender now to thee;
3   In compassion smile upon   me, God   of wisdom, love and might;
4   Je - sus comes! O glory! glo - ry! Now   I feel the blood applied;

I   am wretched, poor, and needy, And   I crave thy sym-pa-thy.
Lord,   to pardon be thy pleasure,   Speak the word and I am   free.
Take   my heart, in pity own   me, And   re - veal thy presence bright.
Let   me tell the blessed sto - ry,   Saved in Christ, the crucified.

CHORUS.

I am waiting at the cross, I am wait-ing at the cross, I am

wait-ing at the cross to be saved; I am wait-ing at the cross, I am

wait-ing at the cross, I am wait-ing at the cross to be saved.

Each Day A Little Nearer.

FAITH WILLIAM.

J. H. TENNEY.

1. Each day a lit-tle near-er To Je-sus would I rise, And find the ser-vice ev-er A glad-ly sweet sur-prise; Tho' what each day is bring-ing My soul may nev-er guess, But to this cross I'm clinging. And on my way I press.

2. And day by day I'm learn-ing That, tho' my earth-ly way, Is oft thro' sha-dows winding, 'Twill lead to per-fect day, Each day I know I'm near-ing His shelt'ring, rest-ful arms; My heart, this thought enfolding, Is safe from earth's alarms.

3. So, trust-ing in His mer-cy And love so mea-sure-less, Each day my soul is ful-ler Of peace and joy-full-ness; Each day while life is giv-en Still near-er would I come, Till from on high my Savior Shall call me, "Child, come home."

Vale Of Beulah.

E. A. HOFFMAN.

JOSEPH GARRISON.

1. { I am pass-ing down the val-ley that they say is so lone,
{ 'Tis to me the vale of Beu-lah, 'tis a beau-ti-ful way,

2. { Not a shad-ow, not a shad-ow ev-er dark-ens the way,
{ And the mu-sic, sweet-ly chant-ed by the heav-en-ly throng,

3. { So I jour-ney with re-joic-ing toward the Cit-y of Light,
{ And I near the o-pen por-tals of the King-dom a-bove,

But I find that all the path-way is with flow'rs o-vergrown;}
For the Sa-vior walks be-side me, my com-pan-ion all day. }

For a ra-diance of rare glo-ry shines up-on it all day: }
Floats in ca-dence down the val-ley, and it cheers me a-long. }

While each day my joy is deeper, and the path grows more bright;}
For this high-way leads to Ca-naan, to the Kingdom of love. }

Chorus.

Vale of Beu-lah! Vale of Beu-lah! Thou art pre-cious to me;

For the love-ly land of Ca-naan In the dis-tance I see.

Holy Spirit! Pity Me.

KING'S HIGHWAY.

E. A. HOFFMAN.

1. Ho - ly Spir - it! pi - ty me, Pierced with grief for grieving
2. Tast-ing that the Lord is good, Pin - ing then for poisoned
3. Oh how light - ly have I slept, With these dai - ly wrongs un-
4. Still Thy com - forts do not fail, Still Thy heal - ing aids a-

Thee, Sins un - num - bered I con - fess, Of ex-
food; At the foun - tains of the skies Crav - ing
wept! Sought thy chid - ings to de - fer, Shunned the
vail; Pa - tient in - mate of my breast, Thou art

ceed - ing sin - ful - ness. Deaf-ness to Thy whispered
crea - ture - ly sup - plies; Chilled de - vo - tions, changed de-
wound - ed Com - for - ter. Woke to ho - ly la - bors
grieved, yet I am blest. Oh be mer - ci - ful to

calls, Rash-ness midst re - mem-bered falls, Tran - sient
sires, Quenched cor - rup - tion's car - lier fires; Sins like
fresh, With the plague - spot in my flesh; An - gel
me Now in bit - ter - ness for Thee! Fath - er,

fears be - neath the rod, Treacherous tri - fling with my God.
these my heart de - ceive, Thee, who on - ly know'st them, grieve.
seemed to hu-man sight, Stood a lep - er in Thy light!
par - don, through Thy Son, Sins a - gainst Thy Spir-it done!

The Warm, Warm Heart Of Jesus.

E. A. HOFFMAN.   R. A. KINZIE.

1. Thy   ten - der heart, dear Je-sus!   Is full of love to   me;
2. O warm, warm heart of Je-sus,   No love like thine so true!
3. O warm, warm heart of Je-sus!   Take one poor sinner in,
4. O warm, warm heart of Je-sus,   So full of sym - pa - thy!

Be - stow on me, Re-deem - er,   That love e - ter - nal - ly.
Each mo - ment, in its ful - ness, It flows to me a - new.
Who longs to share thy mer - cy,   And be redeemed from sin.
With - in thy sa - cred por - tals For ev - er shel - ter me.

Chorus.

O warm, warm heart of Je - sus, So full of love to me!

Come shed a - broad with - in my heart That love e - ter - nal - ly.

Brother, Pray for My Soul.

Words and Music by E. A. HOFFMAN.

1. Brother, pray for my soul to-night! Brother, pray to the Lord of Light!
2. Brother, long I have been astray, Wandered far from my Lord away;
3. Brother, this is my hour of need; Un-to heav-en for mercy plead;

Brother, pray with the spir-it's might! Earnest-ly fer-vent-ly pray!
Weeping, I would re-turn to-day, Pray for me, faithful-ly pray;
God will wel come me then in-deed, Back to his bo-som to-day;

Bear me up to the Father's throne, He has pow'er to save a-lone;
Pray'r to heaven will lift me up, Give me courage and kin-dle hope;
Then my spir-it shall not be lost, Bought at such a tre-men-dous cost,

Ritard. - - - - -

Pray for my soul, Pray for my soul, Earn-est-ly fer-vent-ly pray!
Pray for my soul, Pray for my soul, Earn-est-ly faith-ful-ly pray!
Pray for my soul, Pray for my soul, Plead-ing-ly, trust-ing-ly pray!

Sometime, Somewhere.

E. A. HOFFMAN.

1. Unanswered yet? the pray'r your lips have pleaded In ag - o - ny of
2. Unanswered yet? tho' when you first present - ed This one pe - ti - tion
3. Unanswered yet? nay, do not say un-grant - ed, Perhaps your part is
4. Unanswered yet? Faith cannot be unanswered, Her feet are firm - ly

heart these many years? Does faith begin to fail; is hope de - part - ing,
at the Father's throne, It seemed you could not wait the time of ask - ing,
not yet whol - ly done, The work be-gan when first your pray'r was uttered,
planted on the Rock; A - mid the wild - est storms she stands undaunted,

And think you all in vain those falling tears? Say not, the Fath - er
So urg - ent was your heart to make it known, Tho' years have pass-ed
And God will fin - ish what He has be - gun, If you will keep the
Nor quails be - fore the loudest thun-der-shock, She knows Om-ni - po-

had not heard your pray'r; You shall have your answer sometime, somewhere.
since then, do not despair; God will answer you sometime, somewhere.
in-cense burning there, You shall see his power sometime somewhere.
tence has heard her pray'r, Cries, "It shall be done," sometime, somewhere.

I Want To Be A Worker.

"The laborers are few."—Matt. 9: 37.

I. B.   I. BALTZELL, by per.

1. I want to be a worker for the Lord; I want to love and trust his holy
2. I want to be a worker every day; I want to lead the erring in the
3. I want to be a worker strong and brave; I want to trust in Jesus' pow'r to
4. I want to be a worker; help me, Lord, To lead the lost and erring to thy

word; I want to sing and pray, and be toil-ing ev-'ry day In the
way That leads to heav'n a-bove, where all is peace and love, In the
save; All who will tru-ly come, shall find a hap-py home In the
word That points to joys on high, where pleasures nev-er die In the

Chorus.

vine - yard of the Lord.
king - dom of the Lord.   I will work,   I will
king - dom of the Lord.
king - dom of the Lord.   I will work and pray, I will

pray,   In the vineyard, in the vineyard of the Lord, (of the Lord;) I will
work and pray

work, I will pray, I will la-bor ev'ry day In the vineyard of the Lord.

Wandering Sinner, Return.

E. R. LATTA.   J. H. TENNEY.

1. { Sin-ner, oh, why wilt thou go   Still on thy ru - in - ous way?
   { Why wilt thou hunger and thirst?   Why in the des-ert re-main?

2. { Sin-ner, oh, wander no more!   List to the wel-com-ing sound!
   { Sa-tan would lure thee to death,   Glad-ly thy soul would destroy!

3. { Sin-ner, thy wretchedness see!   Oh, thou art whol-ly un done!
   { He will not turn thee a-way,   If thou respond to his call!

Je - sus hath ransomed thy soul,   Je - sus entreats thee to stay! }
Turn, like the Prodi - gel Son,   Come to thy Sa-vior a - gain! }

On - ly through in-fi - nite love,   Par-don and peace may be found! }
Je - sus would woo thee to life,   Woo thee to life and to joy! }

He will not turn thee a-way,   If thou respond to his call! }
Je - sus who suffered for thee,   Suffered to ransom us all! }

Chorus.

Sin-ner, repent of thy sins!   Cease thy Re-deem-er to spurn!

E'er 'tis for-ev - er too late,   Wan-der-ing sin-ner, re-turn!

Faith Hymn—Trusting Jesus.

R. G. STAPLES, by per.

1. Trusting Je - sus when in sor - row, Trusting him in deep-est
2. Trusting Je - sus on the o - cean, Trusting him up - on the
3. Trusting Je - sus on the mountain, Trusting him in val - ley
4. Trusting Je - sus in the noon-day, When the sun un - cloud-ed
5. Trusting Je - sus when the Spir-it Leaves its ten - e - ment of

gloom; Trusting in affliction's furnace, Trusting him when cares consume.
land; Trusting Christ, who bids the tempest Silent be at his com-mand.
deep, Trusting in the storm's commotion, Trusting Jesus thee to keep.
shines; Trusting Jesus in the midnight, When each earthly hope declines.
clay; Trusting Jesus when the angels Come to bear the soul a-way.

Chorus.

Trusting, trust - ing, ev - er trusting, Trusting Je - sus ev -ery

day; Trusting him in light or darkness, Trusting Je-sus by the way.

We'll Be There.

H. BONAR, Arranged.　　　　　　　　　　　　J. H. TENNEY,

1. Where the earth-fad-ed flow-er shall fresh - en, Freshen
2. Where the morn-ing shall wak-en in glad - ness, And the
3. Where the dear child has found its lost moth - er, And the
4. Where the love-bond is nev-er-more sev - ered, Where no

nev - er, no, nev-er to fade,...... Where the shaded sky
noon the pure joy shall pro - long;...... Where the daylight dis-
moth - er has found her lost child;...... Where the fam-i-lies
part - ing is ev-er-more known,...... We shall meet with the

once more shall brighten, Brighten ne'er to be darkened by shade.
solves in rich fragrance Mid the burst of en-rap-tur-ing song.
once more are gath - er'd That were scattered on this earthly wild.
ho - ly and ransomed By the beau-ti-ful, beauti-ful throne.

Chorus

We'll be there, we'll be there, Crowns unfading and white robes to wear; We'll be

there, we'll be there, In the beau-ty and glo - ry to share.

It Is Brighter Over There.

Mrs. E. W. CHAPMAN.   W. S. MARTIN, by per.

1 The sky with clouds is o-ver-cast, No ray of light is beam-ing
2. Within the city decked with pearls, Where loved ones with the angels
3. The jas-per walls, the crystal sea, The crowns of gold with jewels

fair,   But soft and sweet the whisper low;   It is
are,   No grief disturbs, no tear-drop falls;   It is
rare,   The Lamb, the glo-ry, and the light,   Make it

Refrain.

brighter o-ver there. It is bright-er, It is bright-er, It is
brighter o-ver there.
brighter o-ver there.

over there,   o-ver there,

bright-er o-ver there,   It is bright-er,   It is

o-ver there,   o-ver there,   o-ver there,

bright - er, It is brighter, yes, 'tis brighter over there, over there.

o-ver there.

Don't Keep Jesus Waiting.

C. C. CLINE, by per.

1. Don't keep Je - sus wait-ing, . . . Wait - ing at the door;
2. Don't keep Je - sus wait-ing, ... Wait - ing in the cold;
3. Don't keep Je - sus wait-ing. . . . Wait - ing at the door;

Oft He knocketh soft - ly, Soft - ly ev - er - more;
He will bear you gent - ly. Gent - ly to His fold;
He will be your Sa - vior, E - ven ev - er - more;

I im - plore.

Hear Him, soul, and o - pen, } I implore, I im - plore.
Hear Him, soul. and o - pen, }
Hear Him, soul. and love him. I im - plore.

We Pray for Thy Blessing.

CHARLOTTE MURRAY.

Arranged by J. H. TENNEY.

1. We humb - ly, O Lord, kneel in pray'r at Thy foot - stool, And
2. More gifts we im - plore, Heav'nly Fath - er, O grant them; More
3. More peace 'mid the tur - moil of voic - es around us; More

thirst for a show'r of re - fresh - ing from Thee; Our hearts are so
strength for those du - ties that have to be done; More faith to re -
ea - ger de - sire for Thine ad - vent, O Lord; More light to dis -

§. We know, Ho - ly

hard, they are cold and un - fruit - ful;—Pour down a rich
ly on the help Thou hast prom - ised; More hope to look
cov - er the signs of Thy com - ing; More plea - sure in

Sa - vior, how much Thou hast giv - en, And there - fore we

Fine. Chorus.

bless - ing, life - giv - ing and free.
for - ward to vic - to - ry won. Our wants are so ma - ny, so
read - ing the truths of Thy Word.

ven - ture to ask Thee for more.

D. §.

large, bless - ed Mas - ter, We each have some special desire to im - plore;

Whosoever Will, Let Him Come And Be Saved.

E. A. HOFFMAN.

1. The Spir - it, in our heart, Is whisp-'ring, "Sin-ner, come," The
2. Let him that hear - eth say To all a-bout him, "Come!" Let
3. Yes, who - so - ev - er will, Oh let him free - ly come, And
4. Lo! Je - sus, who in - vites, Declares, "I quick - ly come;" Lord,

Bride, the Church of Christ, proclaims To all his children, "Come!"
him that thirsts for righteous-ness, To Christ, the foun - tain, come!
free - ly drink the stream of life! 'Tis Je - sus bids him come.
e - ven so! we wait thine hour; O blest Re-deem - er, come!

Chorus.

The Spir - it and the Bride say, "Come, sin - ner, come; And

he that is a-thirst, a-thirst let him come, And whosoev-er will, and

who - so - ev - er will, And who - so - ev - er will, let him come and be saved."

The Three Fold Promise.

"ASK— | SEEK— | KNOCK—
and it shall be given you; | and ye shall find; | and it shall be opened unto you."

MARY PACKARD ROLLINS.   J. H. TENNEY.

1. Ask— and the ten - der heart of God, Re-
2. Seek— with an ear - nest soul, and know The
3. Knock— and the Lord of Life for thee Will
4. Oh, roy - al prom - ise, full and free! The

spon - sive to thy plead - ing, Will send a prince - ly
bless - ed - ness of find - ing, A light to guide thy
o - pen wide the por - tal; And rest, and peace, and
King's own sig - net wear - ing, To wea - ry, heav - y-

gift of grace, Thy high - est faith ex - ceed - ing.
stumb - ling steps Through dark - ness thick and blind - ing.
heaven are thine, An her - i - tage im - mor - tal.
la - den souls, A glad e - van - gel bear - ing.

CHORUS.

Oh, golden promise! grand and sweet, As joy-bells softly ring-ing A-

down the a - ges, peace and hope To burdened spir-its bring - ing.

"How shall we escape if we neglect so great salvation."—Heb. 2: 3.

Rev. A. S. Dobbs, D. D.   W. Warren Bentley, by per.

1 I now am so happy in Je-sus' love, No sorrow my song ean control;

I'm wash'd in the fountain which   And Jesus speaks peaoe to my soul.
[flows from His side,

Refrain.

O! why not come to Him now?   O! why not come to him now?

He'll cleanse you, and save you, and fill you with joy; O, why not come to Him now?

2. I know I'm a sinner, a sinner redeemed,
    A brand taken out of the flame!
    I'll let my light shine so that others may see,
    And glorify Jesus' name.—*Chorus.*

3. O, poor wandering sinner, cast off by the way,
    And ready to perish and die,
    Believe, and accept Him, while mercy is near,
    For Jesus is now passing by.—*Chorus.*

4. The way is so simple, the foolish may view,
    The lame and the blind may come too—
    Though your sins are as crimson, he'll welcome you home,
    His blood can make whiter than snow.—*Chorus.*

My Beautiful Home Above.

Words arranged.

A. J. SHOWALTER, by per.

1. { Oh! how my spir - it longs for thee, } Beauti - ful home a - bove!
   { Where I may rest from sorrow free, }

2. { To reach thee safe I dai - ly pray, } Beauti - ful home a - bove!
   { And trav-el in the toilsome way, }

3. { Thy shin-ing walls by faith I see, } Beauti - ful home a - bove!
   { The mansions fair prepared for me, }

With - in the golden gates of light, Arrayed in garments pure and white,
My weary feet are bruis'd and sore, But Jesus' feet were bruis'd before,
Oh! let me keep my longing eyes In - tent - ly fixed up-on the prize,

I'll walk with an-gels fair and bright, In my beautiful home a - bove.
To bring me to the o-pen door Of my beau-ti - ful home a - bove.
Till an-gels bear me to the skies, To my beati - ful home a - bove.

Chorus.

Beau - ti - ful home a-bove.... Beau - ti - ful home a-bove,. ..
Beautiful home, bright home above, Beautiful home, bright home above,

Oh! come and take me, Savior dear, To my beautiful home a - bove.

Come To Him.

ENGLISH.   W. JOHNSON.

1. Ho, ye thirs-ty! Je - sus calls you; Je - sus came to give
2. Wherefore do ye spend your trea - sure Where there is no bread?
3. None can be too Vile for Je - sus, None can be too poor;
4. O his ten-der love and pi - ty! Still He calls to - day;

Wine and milk of full sal - va - tion; Come to Him and live.
On - ly by the liv-ing Sa - vior Dy - ing souls are fed.
By his blood come peace and par - don, Mer-cies ev - er sure.
Nev - er one to Je - sus com - ing Shall be cast a - way.

Chorus.

Who - so - ev - er will may take it, Take His grace and live;

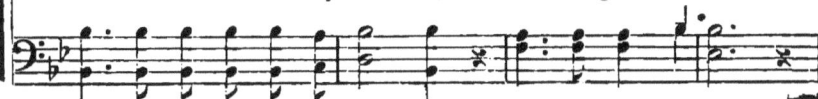

With - out price and without mon - ey, Now the gift receive.

I Am Coming.

J. H. TENNEY.

1. With a heav-y load of woe, Lord, I come, With repentant heart I
2. I will lay my bur-den down at thy feet; See thy child re-turn-ing,
3. Heavy eyes, so tired with weeping, I bring That they scarce can trace the
4. Soon I know the skies will break, Father mine, And the clouds and darkness

come no more to roam; For I know at thy dear feet there is room
heavenly Fa-ther, see! In a voice of tend-er love, low and sweet,
welcomes of thy face; O that I, from sin redeemed, soon may sing
be for-ev-er gone; Look on me with peace and fa-vor di-vine;

Chorus.

For a sin-ner com-ing home. I am com - - ing! I am
Welcome, Lord, and pardon me.
For the gladness of thy grace!
Let the day of mer-cy dawn.

I am coming,

coming, Make the pathway with thy smiling presence bright, fair and bright! I am
I am coming,

com - ing, I am com - ing, Let me be accepted in thy sight.
I am coming, I am coming,

Soft And Low.

Mrs. E. W. Chapman.

J. H. Tenney.

1. Soft and low the gen-tle zephyrs Stir the leaf-lets green;
2. Soft and still the shin-ing dewdrops On the leaves dis-till,
3. Soft and still the morning sunbeams Chase the night a-way,

Soft and low the Spir-it whis - pers Of the joys un-seen.
But the Spir - it's ten-der woo-ing's Lov-ing hearts en-thrill.
So the Spi - rit's bright ef - ful-gence Floods the soul with day.

Chorus.

Gen - tle Spir - it, kind-ly whis - per To our hearts in love;....

Ten-der Spir-it, Christ re - veal - er, Show us joys a-bove.

Closer To Thee.

Words and Melody by Rev. E. H. Long.

Moderato.

1. Draw me, Savior, near - er, Near - er and near - er to Thee;
2. As the eagles soar - ing, High - er and high - er as - cend,
3. As the riv-er flow - ing Dai - ly draws near - er the sea.

Let me see still clearer, All thy love for me. Freed from self, and
Thus, while Thee adoring, Upward I would tend. Far from earth and
Thus may I keep go-ing, Till I'm lost in Thee. E'er ad-vance and

whol-ly Thine, Let me in Thy beauty shine; While I sing, O, may I be
sin a - way, Nearer heaven's perfect day; E - ven now, O, may I be
grow in grace. Till I see Thee face to face; Then I'll sing e - ter-nal-ly,

Rit.   *A tempo.*

Drawn still closer, closer to Thee, Closer, clos-er, clos - er to Thee.
Drawn still closer, closer to Thee, Closer, clos-er, clos - er to Thee.
Drawn still closer, closer to Thee, Closer, clos-er, clos - er to Thee.

I Am The Lord's Forever.

E. A. H.   E. A. HOFFMAN.

1. My glad-some heart these words re - peat; "I am the Lord's for-
2. Too long and far from Christ I strayed, But he for - sook me
3. 'Twas Christ, the Lamb of Cal - va - ry, That loved and sought me
4. I am the Lord's! O bless-ed thought! And he will leave me
5. This is the bur - den of my song; "I am the Lord's for-

ev - er!" And eve - ry time they seem more sweet; Oh,
nev - er; Now walk - ing in the nar - row way, I
ev - er, That broke my chains and set me free; Oh,
nev - er; By Je - sus' blood my soul was bought, And
ev - er!" And naught that earth can of - fer me My

Chorus.

praise his name for-ev - er!
am the Lord's for-ev - er!   { Hal - le - lu - jah! hal - le - lu - jah!
praise his name for-ev - er!   { Hal - le - lu - jah! hal - le - lu - jah!
I am his for-ev - er!
heart from Christ can sever.

{ Light breaks in up - on my soul;
{ Omit............................ } Je - sus blood has made me whole!

Jesus now is Passing by.

Luke 18:37.

Words and music by

R. E. HUDSON.

1. Come, wea-ry sin-ner, to the Cross; The Saviour bids you come; Come,
2. Oh! why de-lay your long re-turn? The Spir-it gently pleads; Come
3. He waits to fill your soul with joy, And all your sins forgive; His

trust-ing in his prec-ious blood; Wait not—there still is room.
to the Cross whereon for you The dy-ing Saviour bleeds.
love for you no tongue can tell; Oh! trust his grace and live!

CHORUS.

Je-sus now is pass-ing by, pass-ing by, pass-ing by,
While he is so ver-y nigh, ver-y nigh, ver-y nigh,

Je-sus now is pass-ing by, I'll go out to meet him.)
While he is so ver-y nigh, I'll go out and greet him. }

WILL YOU AND I BE THERE?

W. F. CHUTE.

ALDINE S. KIEFFER.

1. We know there's a bright and a glo - ri - ous home, A - way in the heav'ns on high,
2. In rai - ments of white, o'er the streets of gold, Beneath a fair, cloud - less sky,
3. From all of the kingdoms of earth they come, To swell the tri - umph - al cry;
4. If we come to him as our Sav - ior now, And up - on his grace re - ly.

Where all the redeemed shall with Je - sus dwell, But will you be there and I?
They walk in the light of the Father's smile, But will you be there and I?
They sing of the Lamb who for us was slain, But will you be there and I?
We'll join in the anthems a - round the throne, In his king - dom by and by.

CHORUS.

Will you and I be there? Will you and I be there? In that

home of love on high, Where saints redeemed shall sing End - less

praise to Christ, our King, O will you be there and I?

From "SING THE GOSPEL." by per.

Jesus Is Able To Save.

E. R. LATTA.

J. H. TENNEY.

1. Sin - ner, un - done thy con-di - tion, Thou art of Sa - tan the
2. If thou wilt seek him in earn - est, Thou his for-give-ness shalt
3. How he, on Cal - va - ry's moun-tain, Prayed for his foes, and for-
4. Think how the migh - ty Re-deem - er Triumphed o'er death and the

slave; Yet thou canst hope for sal-va-tion; Je - sus is a - ble to
have; Thou shalt be freed from thy bondage; Jesus is a - ble to
gave; He will not slight thy pe-ti - tion; Je - sus is a - ble to
grave; Seek him, oh, seek him, or perish! Je - sus is a - ble to

Chorus.

save.......... A - ble to save .... a - ble to
a - ble to safe. A - ble to save,

save, Je - sus is a - ble and will - ing to save, A - ble to

save...... a - ble to save, Je-sus is a - ble and will-ing to save.
A-ble to save.

He Knows Best.

Rev. H. B. HARTZLER.　　　　　　　　　　　　　E. A. HOFFMAN.

1. Let Je - sus lead thee; surely he knows best Which way is saf - est
2 Let Je - sus help thee; surely he knows best What is thy strength, and
3 Let Je - sus teach thee; surely he knows best What lessons thou dost
4. Let Je - sus keep thee; surely he knows best What hidden dangers

for thy ea - ger soul; Walk where he leads and trust him for the rest,
what thy toil and need; Do what thou canst, and leave to him the rest,
need to make thee wise; Receive what he makes plain and leave the rest,
lie a - long thy way; Go, watch and fight and pray, and leave the rest,

Chorus.

And he will bring thee to the high-est goal.
And he will make thy trust thy noblest deed. Let Je - sus save thee;
Till thou shalt see him with im-mor - tal eyes.
To him who is thy ev - er - last-ing stay.

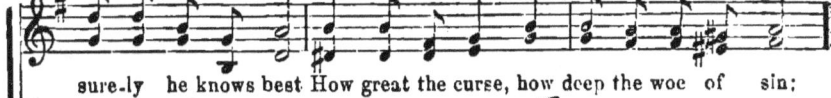

sure-ly he knows best How great the curse, how deep the woe of sin;

Believe, obey, and he will do the rest, And so thy faith eternal life shall win.

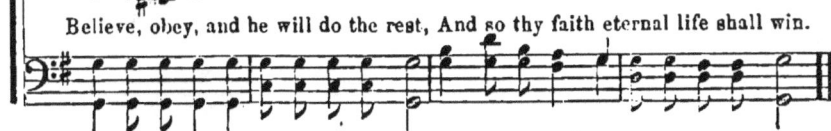

Our Dear Happy Home.

MRS. EMMA PITT.

J. H. TENNEY, by per.

1. Beauteous flowers bloom in heav-en, Flow'rs that never fade a-way,
2. Friends we've lov'd have gone before us, Pass'd the portals of the grave,

All is bright, and calm, and ho-ly, In that land of end-less day:
Sing the hal-le-lu-jah chorus, Vict'ry's ban-ner joy-ful wave:

There temptations can-not harm us, Tears will never dim our eye, There the Savior
There no grief can ev-er en-ter, All is bliss be-yond the sky, We shall see our

REFRAIN.

waits to greet us In that happy home on high. Sweet, sweet home, our dear, happy
bless-ed Savior In that happy home on high.

home, Our sweet, happy home on high, Our dear hap-py home.

Jesus Shall Have It All.

E. A. H.

E. A. HOFFMAN.

1. Je - sus, I hear thee call - ing; "Give me, my son, thy heart!"
2. My whole, though broken heart, Lord, From hence no long-er mine,
3. All of my love, dear Sa - vior, Weak and though cold it be,
4. All of my ser - vice, Mas - ter, All shall be henceforth thine;
5. Sa - vior! this con - se - cra - tion Now in thy book re-cord,

Take thou the gift; 'tis thine, Lord! None else shall share a part.
I lay up - on thine al - tar, And con - se-crate it thine.
All, though so poor and worth-less, Henceforth shall flow to thee.
Help me to keep this cov - 'nant, And all to thee re-sign.
Grant me a faith - ful ser - vice, And then the great re-ward.

Chorus.

My heart I give to thee. Lord, Give it be-yond con-trol;

None else shall share a part, no, Je - sus shall have it all!

Seeking Peace And Rest.

E. A. Hoffman.   E. S. Lorenz.

1. Restless and un-hap-py, Burdened and distressed, Now I come to Jesus,

2. Sin has almost crushed me 'Neath its weight of woe; Now with all my burden,

3. Will the Lord have mercy? Will he pardon me? From my sin and anguish

Chorus.

Seeking peace and rest.

Un - to Christ I go.   If the Lord, my Savior, Will but smile on me,

Will he set me free?

O how ve - ry hap-py My poor soul will be! At the cross I linger,

At the cross I pray, Waiting till the Lord shall Take my sins away.

Only Remembered By What I Have Done.

Dr. Bonar.   WM. W. Bentley. by per.

1. Up and a-way, like the dew of the morning, Soaring from earth to its
2. Shall I be missed if an-oth-er succeed me, Reaping the fields I in
3. On - ly the truth that in life I have spoken, On - ly the seed that on
4. Oh, when the Savior shall make up his jewels, When the bright crowns of re-

home in the sun, Thus would I pass from the earth and its toil - ing,
spring-time have sown? No, for the sow - er may pass from his la-bors,
earth I have sown; These shall pass onward when I am for - got-ten,
joic - ing are won; Then will his faithful and wea - ry dis - ci-ples,

Chorus.

On - ly remembered by what I have done.
On - ly remembered by what he has done. On - ly remembered,
Fruits of the har-vest and what I have done.
All be remembered for what they have done.

On - ly remembered, On - ly remembered by what I have done,

Rit.

Only remembered, Only remembered, Only remembered by what I have done.

Rock of Ages.

J. H. TENNEY, by per.

Bass Solo.

Inst.

1. Rock of a ges! cleft for me; Let me hide myself in thee! Let the
2. Could my zeal no respite know, Could my tears forever flow, All for
3. While I draw this fleeting breath, When my eyelids close in death, When I

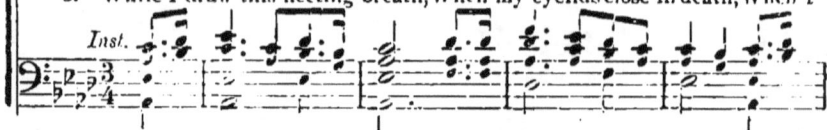

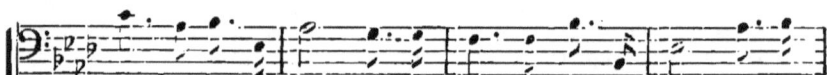

wa - ter and the blood, From thy wound-ed side that flowed, Be of
sin could not a - tone; Thou must save and thou a - lone! Noth-ing
soar to worlds unknown, See thee on thy judgment throne, Rock of

sin the doub - le cure, Save from wrath and make me pure, Save from
in my hand I bring, Sim - ply to thy cross I cling, Sim-ply
A - ges! cleft for me, Let me hide myself in thee, Let me

Rall - en - tan - do.

| 1st time. | 2d time. |

wrath and make me pure.
to thy cross I cling.
(OMIT..........................) hide myself in thee, Let me hide myself in thee!

Jesus, Lover of My Soul.

C. WESLEY. Ps. 9:9. R. E. HUDSON.

Affetuoso.

2. Thou, O Christ, art all I want:
More than all in thee I find:
Raise the fallen, cheer the faint,
Heal the sick and lead the blind.
Just and holy is thy name;
I am all unrighteousness;
False, and full of sin I am;
Thou art full of truth and grace.

3. Plenteous grace with thee is found,—
Grace to cover all my sin:
Make and keep me pure within.
Thou of life the fountain art;
Freely let me take of thee:
Spring thou up within my heart,
Rise to all eternity.

Come, Trust, Pray.

WM. BOECKEL.

1. Come to Je - sus! At his feet in re - pen-tance bow;
2. Trust in Je - sus! Trust his lov - ing and ten - der heart,
3. Pray to Je - sus! He de - light - eth to an - swer prayer;

Come to Je - sus! Tar - ry no long - er now!
And his bless - ing Free - ly he will im-part.
Bow be - fore him! You will find mer - cy there.

Chorus.

He is will - ing to save you, Will-ing to free - ly for-give you; For

Je - sus suffered, yes, Je - sus died To make a-tone-ment for you.

Jesus Said it Would Be So!

E. A. HOFFMAN.

1. When the faithful were as-sem-bled   On   the day of Pen-te-cost,
2. Gold-en shower of con-se-cra - tion, Tongues of fire were on them shed,
3. So when we to-geth-er gath - er   In the prayer-room humbled low,
4. Lo, the power, on us 'tis fall - ing! And our hearts with fire they glow!

Rushed the wind, the place it trembled, Came from heaven the Ho-ly Ghost.
And that ho-ly ded - i - ca - tion, Made an al - tar of each head.
Comes the Pen-te-cost-al pow - er;   Je - sus said it would be so!
God is coming—hal-le - lu - jah! Je - sus said it would be so!

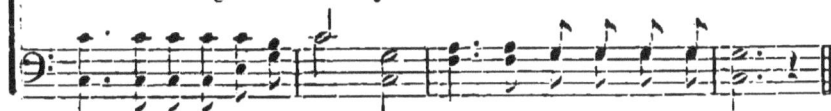

CHORUS.

Je - sus said   it would be   so!   Je - sus said it would be so!

Wondrous prom-ise and ful - fil - ment,   Je - sus said it would be so!

Awake, O Heavenly wind.

THOMAS ROW.

THOS. B. CUNNINGHAM.

Rather Slow.

1. Awake, O heavenly wind, Thou Spirit most divine! Come blow upon thy
2. Come, sweet celestial Dove, In thy reviving gales, And tune our souls to

garden here, And make its graces shine. Let ev-ery fruit-ful plant And
sing the Lamb Whose kindness never fails; Let his sweet name perfume The

Fine.

fragrant spice be seen, To make the garden of our God Most pleasant and serene.
garden of thy care ; And fill our songs and every breath With thy delightful air.

D.S. with the long expected shower, And fill the sacred place.

CHORUS.

O Spirit most divine! In this accepted hour, As on the day of Pentecost, De-

D.S.

scend in all thy pow'r; Come with thy promis'd help, Come with almighty grace, Come

In The Shadow Of The Cross.

E. R. LATTA.　　　　　　　　　　　　　　J. H. TENNEY.

1. There's a place a-bove all oth - ers, Where my spirit loves to be!
2. On the cross my Sa - vior suf-fered, That He might atone for me!
3. When my heart is full of trou - ble, Then I love, on bended knee,
4. Bless-ed Sa-vior, Thou wilt hear me, When I make my earnest plea,

'Tis with - in the sa - cred shad - ow Of the cross of Cal - va - ry!
And I love the bless - ed shad - ow Of the cross of Cal - va - ry!
To approach Him in the shad - ow Of the cross of Cal - va - ry!
If I kneel within the shad - ow Of the cross of Cal - va - ry!

Chorus.

In the shad-ow of the cross, In the shad - ow of the
of the cross,

cross, There my spi-rit loves to be, In the shadow of the cross.
of the cross.

Sweet Paradise.

I. C. MONROE.

E. A. HOFFMAN.

1. How sweet to look beyond the stream, Of death's cold, dismal tide,
2. There heavenly zephyrs gently play Sweeter than breath of even;
3. O blessed home beyond the flood, Where falls no gloomy night;
4. We'll watch, by faith, yon morning star Which now is risen on high,
5. Oh, then what floods of endless light, What heavenly beauties rare,

And catch, by faith, a dis-tant gleam Of joys on Ca - naan's side.
There weary, earth-worn mortals, may Find end - less rest in heav'n.
O glo-rious ci - ty of our God, Where Je - sus is the light.
Un - til those "gates," so long "a-jar," Shall ope for you and I.
Shall burst up-on our ravished sight, In man-sions "o - ver there!"

Chorus.

Sweet Pa-ra - dise! With longing eyes I look to - ward the tomb!

Its por-tals past, I'll be at last With Christ in my sweet home.

Tell Us Something More.

JOSEPHINE POLLARD.   E. ROBERTS, by per.

1. Tell us something more of the love of Jesus, Christian, tell us something more;
2. Tell us something more of the cru-ci-fixion, Tell us how he bled and died;
3. Tell us something more of the Holy City, When they strewed the way with palms;

Tell us how he suffered death for sinners, Tell us of the cross he bore.
Tell us of the blood that ev-er cleanses, Flowing from his wounded side.
Tell us how he gathered lit-tle children In - to his most lov-ing arms.

Chorus.

Tell us, Christian, tell us, Tell us something more

Of the love of Je - sus, Tell us more and more.

COPYRIGHTED 1883, BY J. H. TENNEY.

Nearer Home.

W. J. BOSTWICK.

1. O'er the hills the sun is set - ting, And the eve is draw-ing on,

Slow - ly drops the gen-tle twi - light, For an - oth - er day is gone;

Gone for aye its race is ov - er, Soon the dark-er shades will come,

Still 'tis sweet to know at ev - en, We are one day near-er home.

CHORUS.

Near-er home, near-er home, Near-er our e - ter - nal home,

Near-er home, Near-er home, sweet home.

Near-er home,..... near-er home, We are one day near-er home, nearer home.

Near-er home, dear home. near-er home.

2 Worn and weary, oft the pilgrim,
Hails the setting of the sun,
For his goal is one day nearer,
And his journey nearly done;
Thus we feel when o'er life's desert,
Heart and sandal-sore we roam;
As the twilight gathers o'er us,
We are one day nearer home.

3 Nearer home! yes, one day nearer
To our Father's house on high —
To the green fields and the fountains,
Of the land beyond the sky;
For the heavens grow brighter o'er us,
And the lamps hang in the dome,
And our tents are pitched still closer,
For we're one day nearer home.

Do you know the wondrous story?

J. E. H.   J. E. HALL.

1. { Do you know the wondrous sto-ry, Have you ev-er heard it told?
   { How that Je-sus came from Heaven, (OMIT.)..................... }

CHORUS.

Seeking lost ones from the fold? Do you know the wondrous story? Have you ev-er

heard it told? Do you know the won-drous sto-ry? That with telling ne'er grows old?

2 Have you heard how much he suffered,
Hanging on the cruel tree?
That we all might have salvation
And should live eternally.

3 Is it true that you have heard it?
Have the tidings reached your ear?
Then why not just now believe it,
And find comfort, hope, and cheer.

Be Not Faithless.

JAMES NICHOLSON.   S. WESLEY MARTIN, arranged.
Slowly.

1. Be not faithless, but believing! Thus the Sa - vior speaks to thee;
2. Be not faithless, but believing! Wherefore, Christian, dost thou doubt?
3. Be not faithless, but believing! Will - ing and o - be-dient be;

Those who trust his mighty pow - er, Shall his great sal-va - tion see.
He is wait - ing now to en - ter, Un - be-lief will keep him out.
Place your soul's im-mor-tal in-terests In the Lamb of Cal - va - ry.

Ask, and then by faith receive it, All his gifts are full and free.

In the hour of deep-est darkness, In the time of sore dis-tress,
Take him as your present Sa-vior, From the guilt and pow'r of sin;
Now present your soul and bod-y, As a liv - ing sac - ri - fice;

Call by faith, and Christ will answer, He is al- ways near to bless.
Trust in him this ver-y moment, He can cleanse, and keep you clean.
Those who make this conse-cra - tion, Je-sus sweet-ly sanc - ti - fies

Chorus.   D.S.

Ask for par - don—he will give it; Ask for peace and pur - i - ty;

Wonderful Grace.

MRS. E. W. CHAPMAN.   J. H. TENNEY.

1. Grace suf - fi - cient Je - sus giv - eth, Grace for ev - ery time of need,
2. Grace to fol - low in the dark-ness, Grace to do his ho - ly will,
3. Grace each mo - ment to up-hold me, Grace a-bound-ing, rich and free,
4. Grace o'er ev - ery foe to con-quer, Grace my spir - it to pre - pare,

Grace to bear us thro' earth's tri-als, Grace to trust the Friend in-deed.
Grace to la - bor in the vine-yard, Grace to suf-fer and be still.
Grace to keep me hope-ful, cheer-ful, Grace that I may faith-ful be.
While I run the race with pa-tience, For the man-sions ov - er there.

CHORUS.

Won-der - ful grace of God to me! Won-der - ful mer - cy so rich and free!

Won-der-ful love! O how can it be, He hath bestowed such blessings on me!

Father, Lead Me.

FRANCIS ANSON EVANS.

J. H. TENNEY.

1. Father, lead me, gent - ly lead me, Keep me, keep me near to thee;
2. On the cross, love made thee bear - er Of transgressions not thine own,
3. Though the cup I drink be bitter, Yet, since thou hast made it mine,

Friends I love may oft deceive me— Thou wilt e'er my sol-ace be.
And that love still makes thee sharer In our sor-rows on the throne;
This, thy love, will make it sweeter Than the world's best mingled wine;

Change can ne'er our un - ion sev - er, Death its links may nev - er part;
From thy glo - ry thou art bend-ing Still on earth a pitying eye,
Dark - er days may yet betide me, Sharper ar - rows I may prove,

Yes - ter-day, to - day, for-ev - er Thou the same Re-deem-er art.
And 'mid an - gel songs as—cend-ing, Hearest every mourner's cry.
But the worst will not di-vide me, O my Sa - vior, from thy love!

Now My Heart Is Full Of Rapture.

E. A. HOFFMAN.   REV. I. BALTZELL, by per.

1. Now my heart is full of rap-ture and glad - ness, And my
2. In the downward road of ru - in he found me, Kind - ly
3. In an in-stant all my dark-ness had van - ished, And the
4. Though but late I wan - dered forth in the dark - ness, Far from
5. I am walk-ing in the sun-light of Heav - en, O that

Sa-vior I a-dore and ex - tol, For he banished all my sor-row and
asked me to re-pent and believe, Threw his arms of tender mer - cy a-
heavenly light and peace entered in, I became a child, an heir of the
vir - tue, far from Heaven, and God, Yet today I'm bound with vow to the
words but half my joy could express! I now wear the roy-al robes of the

sad - ness, Washed a-way the stains of sin from my soul.
round me, Whispered, "Child, thy sins I free - ly for - give."
King - dom, And was won - der - ful - ly saved from my sin.
King - dom, Ful - ly rec - on-ciled through Christ's precious blood.
King - dom, Washed and cleansed in Je-sus' blood, I am his.

Chorus.

{ And he dai - - ly walks be-side me,
{ Yes, he leads me and di-rects me,

{ And he dai - ly walks be-side me, And he dai - ly walks be-side me.}
{ Yes, he leads me and di-rects me, Yes, he leads me and directs me.}

1.
And he cheers me with his love by the way, ...   }
2.
And will bring me to his home far a - - way.)

Would you meet me in the Kingdom?

"AMERICAN SPIRITUAL," Arr.

1. O broth-er, will you meet me, On Ca-naan's bright and beau-ti - ful shore?
2. What is your hope, my broth-er? Is Christ the on - ly trust of your heart?
3. O bear the cross, my broth - er, Walk dai - ly in the path-way of light,

In heav - en will you meet me, When the toils and sor-rows of this life are o'er?
To - day, if He should call you, Could you an-swer I am read y to de-part?
And when the Sa-vior calls you, In the King-dom you shall walk with him in white.

CHORUS.

If in Heav - en you would meet me, You must wash your gar-ments white in the

Savior's blood, You must wash them, you must cleanse them, In the Savior's precious blood.

What will you do in that Day?

T. B. W.

T. B. WEAVER.

Tenderly. SOLO OR DUET.

1. Lis-ten. oh! lis-ten to Je - sus, Tender-ly asking your heart,
2. Christ is a ref-uge for sin - ners. Flee to the arms of his love;
3. Toiling for wealth that will per-ish, Charmed with the toys that decay,
4. Think of the loved ones in Heaven, In yonder cit - y of Light,

Will-ing to res-cue and save you, And his rich grace to impart!
If you neg-lect this sal - va - tion, How can you meet him above?
Blinded by sin and by fol - ly,.... Sinning from day un-to day,
Waiting for you at the por - tal, What, if your soul take its flight?

Oh! if his calls are all slighted,.... And in your sins you still go,
Can you not give up your pleas ures, Turn from earth's trifles a way?
Sin - ner, just think of the wa - ges You for your sin shall receive!
Would you be read y to greet them, Anxious the gates to pass through?

What will you do in the judgment. Wonder-ful day of great woe?
Oh! if you cling to your i - dols, What will you do in that day?
Turn to the dear, lov-ing Sa - vior, Hum-bly con fess and be-lieve!
If you have no hope in Je - sus, Sinner, then, what will you do?

CHORUS.

Oh! what will you do?.... Oh! what will you do?....

Repeat pp.

Oh! what will you do..... In that wonder - ful, **won-der-ful** day?

Whosoever Believeth.

"For God so loved the world, that He gave His only begotten Son, that whosoever believeth in Him should not perish, but have everlasting life." John 3: 16.

Rev. FREDERICK DENISON.   W. WARREN BENTLEY, by per.

1. From Calvary's mountain sounding, What lov - ing words we hear,
2. O! seek this great sal-va - tion, And cast out ev - ery . sin,

The love of God a-bound - ing, Dis-pel - ing all our fear.
The souls' e-man - ci - pa - tion, By power Divine with - in.

Refrain..

O! Bro - ther, be-lieve it, O! Bro - ther, receive it:

Who - so - ev - er believ - eth Hath ev - er - last - ing life.

3. Whoe'er my Word believeth,
   We hear the Savior say,
   A pardon full receiveth,
   All sins are washed away.

4 O! Brother come and trust Him,
   O! come to Him to-day,
   He's waiting to receive you,
   Why longer then delay?

Be Thou My Help.

Psalms CXLVI-5.   "Happy is he that hath the God of Jacob for his help, whose hope is in the Lord his God."

C. E. P.   Music by Chas. Edw. Prior, by per.

1. Be Thou my *help*, my joy   in   trib - u - la-tion— O God of   Ja - cob,
2. Be Thou my *friend*, when earthly friends forsake me—O God of   Ja - cob,
3. Be Thou my *all*, when nearing death's dark billow—O God of   Ja - cob,

hear me from a-bove; And may my soul in ev -'ry sore temp-ta-tion Look
be Thou at my side, And may Thy ev - er-blessed-Spir-it make me More
hold me in Thine arms; Dispel all fear, and let my dy - ing pil - low Dis-

Chorus.

up   to   Thee, with con - fi-dence and   love.
close ly lean on Thee, my lov - ing guide.   Shield and de- fend, on
play Thy glo - ry, and re-flect Thy charms.

Thee   I   de-pend, My help and   my strength are from Thee,

Guard and provide—I'll ever confide, Till Thou shalt from sin set me free.

Don't Forget To Pray.

E. R. LATTA.   J. H. TENNEY.

1. E - ven when thy hands are bu - sy, With the labors of the day,
2. When the mind with care is burdened, Or with joy doth overflow,
3. When the breezy morn is shining, When doth sink the evening sun,
4. When the heart is crushed with sorrow, On the Lord thy burdens lay!

Se - cret - ly thy heart can wor - ship—Thou canst to the Father pray!
Still in secret thou canst worship—Well the Lord thy thoughts doth know!
Se - cret - ly thy soul can worship— Thou canst pray, Thy will be done.
Lift thy soul to Him in wor ship— Thou canst ever hope and pray!

Chorus.

What - so - ev - er thou neg - lect - est, Do not this de - lay!

What-so-ev-er thou for-get - test, Don't for-get to pray!

The Land is Drawing Near.

FAITH MILMAN.   REV. L. WHITE.

1. There's a land beyond the riv-er, Of its beauties we are told, All its
2. 'Tis the land of light and glo-ry,'The the bright immortal shore, Where the
3. There a crown of life is giv - en, To each sol-dier of the cross, Who has

walls are made of jas - per, And its streets of shin - ing gold; There the
tree of life is bloom-ing, In the sweet for - ev - er more; There the
lived for God and heav - en, Who has count ed earth but dross, And a

good of ev-ery na - tion, Shall be gath ered home at last, Robed in
anthems loud are swelling, And the crys-tal wa - ters lave, And the
robe of shin-ing splen-dor, And a palm of vic - tor - y; And the

CHORUS.

garments of salvation When the storms of life are past. Rejoice! rejoice!
saints are ev-er praising Christ the mighty one to save. Rejoice! rejoice! the
saved will reign with Jesus thro' a long e ter-ni ty.

land is draw-ing near; The pearly gates are lifting. And the throne will soon appear.

Copyright, 1883, by E. A. HOFFMAN.

Jesus, Save Me Now.

E. A. H.

E. A. HOFFMAN.

1. Lord, my heart is bruised and bleed - ing With the wounds of sin;
2. I am bowed in grief and sor - row, Bur - dened and op - prest!
3. Let the bonds of sin be brok - en, Free - ly all for - give!
4. Come, dear Sav-ior, come and bless me, With thy match less grace;
5. Why not now, dear Lord, for - give me Thro' thy grace di - vine?

For thy mer - cy I am plead-ing, Come and make me clean.
Come ere dawns an - oth - er mor - row, Bring me peace and rest.
Let the word of power be spok - en, That shall bid me live.
Turn to me thy heart of mer - cy, And thy smil - ing face.
Why not now, dear Lord, re-ceive me As a child of thine?

CHORUS.

All my guilt and sin con - fess - ing, At thy feet I bow,

I am wait - ing for thy bless-ing, Je - sus, save me now!

A Harp, a Robe, a Crown.

REV. L. WHITE.   REV. E. STINCHCOMB.

1. Oh, give me a harp on the bright hills of glo - ry, When
2. Oh, give me a crown in the fade - less for - ev - er, Be-
3. Then give me a robe from the hands of my Sav - ior, That's

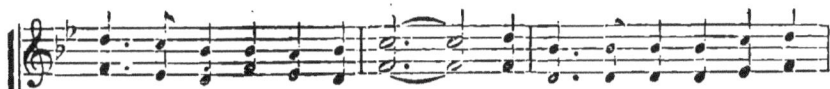

life and its la-bors are o'er,........ To sing with the an - gels the
yond where the pearly gates stand,...... To shine on for - ev - er, in
washed and made white in his blood;...... I'll sing the glad song of re-

theme of the ho - ly, Who dwell on the glo - ri - fied shore.........
glo - ri - fied splendor, With saints all im-mor - tal and grand..........
demption for - ev - er, And dwell in the land of our God.........

CHORUS.

Oh! the song that we'll sing, To the Savior, our King, When life and its la - bors are o'er

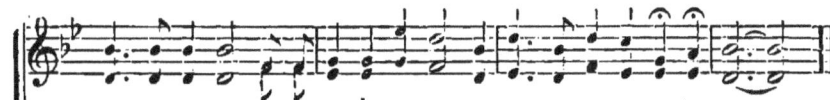

Is the song of his love, And with angels a-bove, We'll dwell in his light evermore!

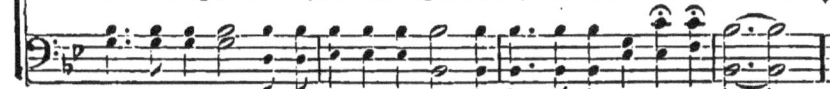

Go Work in My Vineyard.

L. W.   REV. L. WHITE.

1. The sin - ner is gone from the Father astray; He wanders from God and the
2. A storm, wild and raging, is soon coming on; How deep-ly the loud thunders
3. Go res-cue the per-ish-ing, sighing with grief; Go tell them the story of
4. Oh! what will become of the wand'rer, astray, Re-turn ing, a-las! but too

light ;   Far out in the dark he is lost to-day, With no one to guide him aright.
roll! Make haste to thy work ere the day be gone; No time, then, for saving a soul.
love; Go tell them of Jesus who sends relief In mercy from heaven a-bove.
late ? The cry of his doom he will hear "away! The Master hath closed up the gate."

CHORUS.

O ye servants of God, a - way, a - way! "Go work in my vineyard to -

day!" Lead the lost by the hand to Immanuel's land, "Go work" is thy Father's command.

In the Cross of Christ I Glory.

Gal. 6 : 14.

J. H. TENNEY.

1. In the Cross of Christ I glo - ry, Tow'ring o'er the wrecks of time;
2. When the woes of life o'ertake me, Hopes deceive and fears annoy;
3. Bane and blessing, pain and pleasure, By the Cross are sanctified;

All the light of sa - cred sto - ry Gathers round its head sublime.
Never shall the Cross forsake me; Lo! it glows with peace and joy.
Peace is there that knows no measure, Joys that thro' all time abide.

CHORUS.

I am cling-ing to the Cross,
I am cling-ing, cling - ing, cling-ing to the Cross,

I am cling-ing to the Cross,
I am cling-ing, cling - ing, cling-ing to the Cross,

Cling-ing, cling-ing, Yes, I'm cling-ing to the Cross.
Yes, I'm clinging, clinging to the Cross.

Washed and Cleansed.

E. A. A.   E. A. HOFFMAN.

1. O won-der-ful depth of God's won-der-ful love! Its ful-ness I
2. O won-der-ful heights of God's won-der-ful love, En-thrilling my
3. O won-der-ful breadths of this riv-er of love! From hence I would

know, and its sweet-ness I prove; Christ brought me such wealth, such a
soul with the joy from a-bove! Such rest as the Lord on his
nev-er a mo-ment re-move; Its wa-ters I'll drink, and I'll

treasure of peace, My soul is o'erwhelmed in a sea of pure bliss.
saints doth be-stow, No sin-ner un-saved or un-pardoned can know.
here make my rest; For lean-ing on Christ I am per-fect-ly blest.

CHORUS.

For my Savior has washed me in the fountain of his blood. He has washed me and
Hal-le-lu-jah, he saves me! I am reconciled to God! Let me (OMIT.........

cleansed me in the flowing, crimson flood,..
.... praise him for-ev-er, A-men!)

Copyright, 1883, by. E. A. HOFFMAN.

I Am With Thee Every Hour.

Arranged from a 'Jubilee Song," by J. H. T.

1. { I am with thee ev-ery hour, O ransomed one, For too
I am with thee ev-ery hour, trust thou in Me, For My
2. { I am with thee ev-ery hour, I know thy care, I will
I am with thee ev-ery hour, My strength is thine, Thou the
3. { I am with thee ev-ery hour, till life's work done, I shall
I am with thee ev-ery hour, and Heav-en waits To throw

CHORUS.

long the way, and dark, for thee a-lone: }
love un-change-a-ble is pledged to thee. }
cheer thy troub-led heart, thy bur-dens bear; }   . I am
ten-der branch, and I the liv-ing vine. }
bear thee hence to stand be-fore the throne: }
o-pen wide for thee its pear-ly gates. }

with thee, yes, I'm with thee, with thee, Ev-ery hour I'm with thee, with thee,

Thou art mine, for thee my life I gave!... I am with thee, yes, I'm with thee,

with thee,

Ev-ery hour I'm with thee,   With my love I'll guard, and guide, and save!

with thee,

I AM SWEETLY SAVED IN JESUS.

"Who loved me, and gave Himself for me." —GAL. 2:20.

MRS. M. E. BLISS WILSON.   W. W. BENTLEY, by per.

1. Oh! the wondrous love that res-cued, My poor soul from guilt and sin;
2. In my wretch-ed-ness I wan-dered, Seek-ing how to ease my mind;
3. 'Twas the Spir-it whis-pered to me, Seek in Christ thy rest and peace;
4. Now I know that Je-sus saves me, Fill-ing all my soul with love;

Oft I heard the Spir-it knock-ing, Then I wel-comed Je-sus in.
Though I tried all earth-ly pleas-ure, Peace and rest I could not find.
And with earn-est-ness I sought him, And he gave my soul re-lease.
Un-to him be praise and glo-ry, Both in earth and heav'n a-bove.

REFRAIN.

I am sweet-ly saved in Je-sus, Glo-ry, glo-ry fills my soul,

I am sweet-ly saved in Je-sus, And His blood has made me whole.

For You and for Me.

Words and Music by WILL. L. THOMPSON.

Very slow.

1. Soft - ly and ten-der - ly Je-sus is call-ing, — Call-ing for you and for me.
2. Why should we tarry when Je-sus is pleading, — Pleading for you and for me?
3. Time is now fleet-ing, the moments are passing, — Passing from you and from me.
4. O for the won-der - ful love he has promised, — Promised for you and for me.

See on the por-tals He's wait-ing and watch-ing, —
Why should we lin - ger and heed not His mer-cies, —
Shad - ows are gath - er - ing, deathbeds are com - ing, —
Tho' we have sinn'd He has mer - cy and par - don, —

REFRAIN.

Watch-ing for you and for me.
Mer - cies for you and for me?
Com - ing for you and for me.
Par-don for you and for me.

Come home, come home,

cres. *rit.* *p* *pp*

Ye who are wea-ry, come home; Ear - nest-ly, ten-der - ly,

ritard. *pp*

Je - sus is call-ing, — Call-ing, O sin-ner, come home.

Come, Holy Spirit.

I. WATTS

E. A. HOFFMAN.

1. Come, Ho - ly Spirit, heaven - ly dove! With all thy quick'ning pow'rs; Kin-
2. Look how we grov-el here be-low Fond of these earth-ly toys! Our
3. In vain we tune our for-mal songs; In vain we strive to rise; Ho -
4. Dear Lord, and shall we ev - er live At this poor dy-ing rate— Our
5. Come, Ho - ly Spirit, heaven-ly dove! With all thy quick'ning pow'rs; Come

dle a flame of sa-cred love In these cold hearts of ours.
souls, how heav - i - ly they go To reach e - ter - nal joys.
san - nas lan-guish on our tongues, And our devo - tion dies.
love so faint, so cold to thee, And thine to us so great.
shed a - broad a Savior's love, And that shall kin-dle ours.

CHORUS.

O come, O come, Re - fin - ing Spir - it,
O come, O come,

come! Come with thy grace and ho-li-ness, Come and make our hearts thy home.

Copyright, 1883, by E. A. HOFFMAN.

Hallelujah, What a Savior!

BEULAH.

BENJ. F. NYSEWANDER, by per.

With expression.

1. { Once my eyes.... saw noth-ing comely,......, In the low - ly
All His grace..... was hid-den from me,..... By the clouds... of

CHORUS.

Naz - a - rene:..... }
sin be-tween;... }
Hal - le - lu - jah, hal - le-lu - jah!......

I was blind, but now I see; Hal - le - lu - jah,

Ritard...

hal - le - lu - jah! Je - sus wrought the cure for me.

2 Once my dull ears found no music,
In His tender, pleading voice ;
Now He speaks, and each low whisper
Makes my trembling heart rejoice.
Hallelujah, hallelujah !
His dear word has made me free ;
Hallelujah, hallelujah !
O, what boundless liberty !

3 Once my robes, by sin polluted,
Were as filthy rags unclean ;
In the great King's royal presence,
I could never thus be seen ;
Hallelujah, hallelujah !
I am whiter now than snow;
Hallelujah, hallelujah !
Jesus' blood has made me so.

4 Once I roamed in deserts dreary,
Sought in vain a place of rest ;
Now my soul, no longer weary,
Leans, entranced, upon His breast ;
Hallelujah, hallelujah !
Blessedness beyond degree !
Hallelujah, hallelujah !
Jesus is a rest for me.

5 Hallelujah, what a Savior !
Half His love was never told ;
I have found His royal favor,
Richer treasure far than gold.
Hallelujah, hallelujah !
Praise Him, O my ransomed soul !
Hallelujah, hallelujah !
While eternal ages roll.

The Fountain.

REV. S. Y. HARMER. J. H. LESLIE, by per.

Fine.

1 { Oh, come to the fountain of cleansing with me, The wonderful fountain of blood ;
Its streams are now flowing so plenteous and free, Come, plunge in the rich purple flood;

2. { Believ - ing in Je-sus will gladness impart, Be - liev-ing on Je-sus a - lone;
What-ev - er dis-tresses or bur-dens the heart, Will all in a moment be gone.

3. { Come, then, to this fountain and do not de-lay, Be cleansed from pollution and sin ;
The wa-ters are flow - ing, then why should you stay, Oh, wash in the blood of the Lamb!

D. C. Then fly to the fountain with all thy dis-tress, The joys of sal - va - tion to know.
D. C. Whose spir-it of cleansing doth make us complete ; All praise to Immanuel's name!
D. C. Then trust in His mercies and promises true, And wash in the all-cleansing blood,

D.C.

Its vir - tues are heal-ing, I know, I confess, His blood washes whiter than snow;
All glo - ry to Je - sus, we'll gladly re-peat, With joy His forgiveness pro-claim,
Sal - va - tion and glo - ry and hon-or are due, For blessings so rich-ly be-stowed;

Precious Blood of Jesus.

Words and Music by FRANCES RIDLEY HAVERGAL.

1. Pre-cious, pre-cious blood of Je - sus, Shed on Cal - va - ry, Shed for reb - els,
2. Pre-cious, pre-cious blood of Je - sus, Let it make thee whole; Let it flow in
3. Tho' thy sins are red like crimson, Deep in scar - let glow, Je - sus' pre-cious
4. Now tho ho - li - est with boldness, We may en - ter in, For the o-pened

D. S.—O believe it,

Chorus.

Fine. *D.S.*

shed for sin-ners, Shed for me,
migh - ty cleansing, O'er thy soul. Precious, precious blood of Jesus, ev-er flowing free!
blood will wash thee White as snow.
fount-ain cleaneth From all sin,

O receive it, 'Tis for thee.

Hark! a Thrilling Voice is Sounding.

"Now it is high time to awake out of sleep."

W. H. HAVERGAL.

1. Hark! a thrilling voice is sounding; "Christ is nigh," it seems to say;
2. Wak-ened by the sol - emn warning, Let the earth-bound soul a-rise;

"Cast a - way the dreams of darkness, O ye children of the day!"
Christ, her Sun, all ill dis - pell - ing, Shines up on the morn - ing skies.

Cho. Hal - le - lu - jah! hal - le - lu - jah! Praise the ev - er - last - ing King.

3. Lo! the Lamb, so long expected,
Comes with pardon down from heaven;
Let us haste. with tears of sorrow,
One and all to be forgiven. Cho.

4. And when next he comes with glory,
And the world is wrapped in fear,
With his mercy may he shield us,
And with words of love draw near. Cho.

My Sacrifice.

HARRIET McEWEN KIMBALL, alt.

E. A. HOFFMAN.

1. Savior, is there anything I have failed, failed to bring?
Lies my offering at thy feet, [omit.................................] In - com - plete?

2. Lord, bethink thee, I am poor,
Scant and small is my store;
At thy feet my all I pour,
What can I more?

3. Since thou, Lord, hast deigned to ask
O how sweet is the task,
Though the gift be poor, to bring
Everything?

4. Savior, is there anything,
I have now failed to bring?
Lies my offering incomplete
At thy feet?

5. Savior, O do not despise
This, my poor sacrifice!
Take the gift I bring to thee,
And bless me.

94

Have You Heard the News?

Words and Music by REV. SAMUEL ALMAN.

1. Have you heard the news proclaimed, How the wand'rers are reclaimed,
2. Have you heard the tid - ings go, In - to homes of want and woe,
3. Have you in the pris - on cell, Heard those sweetest notes which tell
4. Let your voic - es thus proclaim, In the haunts of sin and shame,

And the blind, and halt, and maimed, Have a friend in Je - sus?
There to let poor sin - ners know, What a Friend is Je - sus?
From condemned ones, all is well, When they trust in Je - sus?
Free forgiveness in his name, Prec-ious name of Je - sus?

CHORUS.

1st. 2d.

A friend in need, a friend indeed, Have you this friend in Jesus? Je-sus?

Copyright by REV. S. ALMAN.

Wash Me in the Blood of the Lamb.

E. A. H.   E. A. HOFFMAN.

1st. 2nd.

1. { I know I am un - worth - y Thy child and heir to be, ...
   { But thou hast died for sinners, And therefore, Lord, for .... me.
2. { Nothing of price or mer - it Have I to bring to thee, ...
   { Yet, as a need - y sin - ner, Dear Savior, welcome .... me.
3. { From sin and con-dem-na-tion, Lord, set me fully free; ....
   { Thou art the only Sav - ior, For help I come to .... thee.

Wash Me in the Blood of the Lamb.—Concluded.

E. A. H.

CHORUS.

E. A. HOFFMAN.

Then wash me, and I shall be whiter than snow, Wash me and I shall be whiter than snow,

Wash me in the blood of the Lamb, And I shall be whit-er than snow.

Too Late—No Room!

MRS. SUE M. O. HOFFMAN.

J. H. TENNEY.

Slowly, Earnestly.

1. Too late—no room! The "Lamb's bright hall of song" Is clos'd for-ev - er
2. While down the slope of hills the day de-clin'd, Thou in thine ease and
3. Did'st thou not see the shadows rush-ing by, And hear the Spirit's
4. A - las! a-las! the banquet was for thee, The bridegroom bade thee
5. Now closed for-ev - er is the door, and barred; Tis vain to cry: Oh

REFRAIN.

'gainst the giddy throng.
fol - ly hast reclined.
earn-est, plead-ing cry? "Too late—no room!" Ye cannot enter now?
come, and love was free.
let me in, my Lord!

Jesus will give you rest.

FANNY CROSBY.   JOHN R. SWEENEY, by per.

1. { Will you come, will you come with your poor brok-en heart,
   { Lay it down at the feet of your Sav - ior and Lord,

D. C. *why won't you come in sim-ple, trusting faith,*

1st.   **2nd.** **Fine.** CHORUS.

Burden'd and sin - op - pressed?   } O hap-py rest,
Jesus will give you [omit.]   rest.

Je - sus will give you [omit.] *rest.*

D. C.

sweet, happy rest! Je - sus will give you rest,   Oh!

hap py rest.

2 Will you come, will you come?
  There is mercy for you,
Balm for your aching breast;
Only come as you are,
  And believe on his name,
Jesus will give you rest.

3 Will you come, will you come?
  How he pleads with you now!
Fly to his loving breast;
And whatever your sin
  Or your sorrow may be,
Jesus will give you rest.

Vaughn.   8s & 4s.

FOR MALE VOICES.   J. H. TENNEY. by per.

1. There is a calm for those who weep, A rest for wea - ry pilgrims found;
2. The storm that sweeps the wintry sky No more disturbs their deep repose;
3. I long to lay this painful head And aching heart beneath the soil;

They soft - ly lie, and sweetly sleep, Low in the ground.
Than summer eve - ning's lat-est sigh, That shuts the rose.
To slum-ber, in that dreamless bed, From all my toil.

Fill Me Now.

REV. E. H. STOKES. D. D.   JNO. R. SWENEY, by per.

1. Hov - er o'er me, Ho - ly Spir - it; Bathe my trembling heart and brow;
2. Thou can'st fill me gra-cious Spir - it, Tho' I can-not tell Thee how;
3. I am weak-ness, full of weak-ness; At thy sacred feet I bow;
4. Cleanse and com-fort; bless and save me; Bathe, oh, bathe my heart and brow;

S.   *Fine.*

Fill me with thy hal-low'd pres-ence, Come, Oh, come and fill me now.
But I need Thee, great-ly need Thee, Come, Oh, come and fill me now.
Blest, di-vine, e - ter - nal Spir - it, Fill with pow'r and fill me now.
Thou art com - fort - ing and sav - ing, Thou art sweet-ly fill-ing now.

D. S. Fill me with Thy hal-low'd pres-ence, Come, oh, come and fill me now.

REFRAIN.   D.S.

Fill me now, fill me now, Je - sus, come and fill me now.

NOT FAR FROM THE KINGDOM.

"Now is the day of salvation."—2 Cor. 6:2.

ENGLISH.   A. J. SHOWALTER.

1. Not far, not far from the kingdom, Yet in the shadow of sin; How
2. Not far, not far from the gateway, Where voices whisper and wait; But
3. Catching the strains of the music, Floating so sweetly a - long; Tho'
4. Out in the dark and the danger, Out in the night and cold; Tho'

ma - ny are com-ing and go - ing, How few are en - ter-ing in.
fear-ing to en - ter in bold - ly, They lin-ger still at the gate.
knowing the song they are sing - ing, Yet join-ing not in their song.
he is now long-ing to lead them So kind-ly in - to the fold.

CHORUS.

Not far, not far from the kingdom, Yet ling'ring still at the gateway; Oh,

wait not to get near - er; But en - ter while you may.

Copyright, 1883, by E. A. HOFFMAN.

Gathering Home.

Rev. 20; 12.

I. B.

REV. I. BALTZELL, by per.

1. We'll all gath-er home in the morn-ing, On the banks of the bright jasper
2. We'll all gath-er home in the morn-ing, At the sound of the great ju bi-
3. We'll all gath-er home in the morn-ing, Our bless-ed Redeem-er to

sea; We'll meet all the good and the faith-ful; What a gath'ring that will be!
lee; We'll all gath-er home in the morn-ing; What a gath'ring that will be!
see; We'll meet with the friends gone before us; What a gath'ring that will be!

CHORUS.

What a gath - 'ring, gath - 'ring,
What a gath - 'ring that will be, that will be, What a

gath-'ring that will be! What a gath - 'ring,
that will be! While the an-gels sing, we'll

gath - 'ring, What a gath - 'ring that will be!
all gath - er home!

We shall Rest in the Cool of the Day.

F. A. EVANS. A. J. SHERWALTER, by per.

1. On the breast of the mighty Je - ho - vah We have learned in all trust to repose,
2. For a light shineth down thro' the shadows And the narrow gate pathway we see,

For His mercy will carry us o - ver, Tho' the legions of darkness oppose;
Lying straight o'er the thorn mantled meadows, And it waiteth for you and for me;

Tho' the shadows of grief gather o'er us, And the sun shineth dim on the day;
And we gather his soul cheering sto-ry, From the saints who have trodden the way;

He will send the cloud-pillar before us, He will lead us himself on the way.
Where the Lord taketh up to His glo - ry, They shall rest in the cool of the day.

CHORUS.

There we'll rest, sweetly rest, Rest in the cool of the day.
There we'll rest, sweetly rest,

There we'll rest,   sweetly rest,   Rest. in the cool of the day.
There we'll rest   sweetly rest,

In Heaven We'll Meet Again.

REV. W. W. SHULER.   MISS CALLIE SWARTZ.

1. An-oth - er day of toil has fled, And mul-ti - tudes have gone To
2. How ma - ny bless-ings rich and choice, On earth were kindly giv'n ; But
3. The past with so much mercy strew'd, Is with its life work gone ; The
4. We ren-der grate-ful thanks to God For his pre serv-ing care, Whose

CHORUS.

join the si-lent, sleeping dead, And wait the judgment morn.
these will not compare with joys That greet the sav'd in heav'n. Farewell ! Fare-
re-cord of its good or ill Is at the Fa-ther's throne.
grace will bring us safely to The mansions o - ver there.

Rit..................

well ! we here awhile remain ; Farewell ! Farewell ! In heav'n we'll meet again

Copyright, 1883, by. E. A. HOFFMAN.

102

WEBB.

O ye who seek the Saviour, look up in
    faith and love,
Come up into the sunshine, so bright and
    warm above !
No longer tread the valley, but clinging
    to his hand,
Ascend the shining summits, and view
    the glorious land.

Our harp-notes should be sweeter, our
    trumpet-tones more clear,
Our anthems ring so grandly that all the
    world must hear,
Oh! royal be our music, for who hath
    cause to sing,
Like these, the Lord's redeemed ones, the
    children of the King !

In full and glad surrender we give our-
    selves to Thee,
Thine utterly, and only, and evermore to
    be.
O Son of God, who lov'st us, we will be
    thine alone,
And all we are, and have, Lord, shall
    henceforth be thine own !

DENNIS.

WE meet now in thy name,
    We plead thy promise, Lord,
Thy presence with us, Lord, we claim
    According to thy word.

Show us thy hands, thy side,
    And as those wounds we see,
May each exclaim, For me Christ died!
    He lives again for me !

Open each mind and heart,
    To understand thy word,
That we may see in every part,
    The Christ, the Lamb of God.

Breathe on each waiting soul,
    And may we all receive
The Holy Ghost, in us to dwell,
    Our hearts ne'er more to leave,

Believing, we rejoice
    Our risen Lord to see,
And say with gladsome heart and voice,
    My Lord! my God! to thee.

Fill us with peace and joy,
    Thou, who for us wast slain;
We'll others tell and others bring
    To meet thee here again.

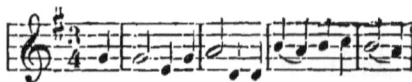

O MOURNER in Zion, how blessed art thou,
    For Jesus is waiting to comfort thee now,
Fear not to rely on the word of thy God,
Step out on the promise,—get under the
    blood.

O ye that are hungry and thirsty, rejoice!
For ye shall be filled. Hear ye not that sweet
    voice
Inviting you now to the banquet of God?
Step out on the promise,—get under the
    blood.

Who sighs for a heart from iniquity free ?
O, poor troubled soul ! there's a promise for
    thee ;
There's rest, weary one, in the bosom of God;
Step out on the promise,—get under the
    blood.

The promise don't save, though each promise
    is true ;
'Tis the blood we get under that cleanses us
    through ;
It cleanses us now, give the glory to God !
We rest on the promise,—we're under the
    blood.

THE Holy Ghost is come:
    We feel his presence here;
Our hearts would now no longer roam,
    But bow in filial fear.

This tenderness of love,
    This hush of solemn power,
'Tis heaven descending from above
    To fill this favour'd hour.

Earth's darkness all has fled,
    Heav'ns light securely shines,
And ev'ry heart divinely led,
    To holy thought inclines.

No more let sin deceive,
    Nor earthly cares betray :
Oh ! let us never, never grieve
    The Comforter away,

The Wondrous Gift.

GRACE 'tis a charming sound,
    Harmonious to the ear;
Heaven with the echo shall resound,
    And all the earth shall hear,

REF.—Saved by grace alone,
This is all my plea;
Jesus died for all mankind,
And Jesus died for me.

Grace first contrived a way
To save rebellious man;
And all the steps that grace display,
Which drew the wondrous plan.

Grace taught my roving feet
To tread the heavenly road:
And new supplies each hour I meet,
While pressing on to God.

Grace all the work shall crown,
Through everlasting days;
It lays in heaven the topmost stone,
And well deserves our praise.

I Love Thy Kingdom.

I LOVE thy kingdom, Lord,
The house of thine abode,
The Church our blest Redeemer saved
With his own precious blood:

I love thy Church, O God!
Her walls before thee stand,
Dear as the apple of thine eye,
And graven on thy hand.

Beyond my highest joy
I prize her heavenly ways:
Her sweet communion, solemn vows,
Her hymns of love and praise.

Sure as thy truth shall last,
To Zion shall be given
The brightest glories earth can yield,
And brighter bliss of heaven.

How Sweet the Name.

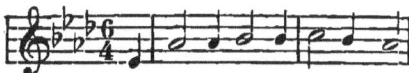

HOW sweet the name of Jesus sounds
In a believer's ear:
It soothes his sorrows, heals his wounds,
And drives away his fear.

It makes the wounded spirit whole,
And calms the troubled breast;
'Tis manna to the hungry soul,
And to the weary rest.

Jesus, my Shepherd, Saviour, Friend;
My Prophet, Priest, and King;
My Lord, my Life. my Way, my End,—
Accept the praise I bring.

I would thy boundless love proclaim
With every fleeting breath:
So shall the music of thy name
Refresh my soul in death.

O Holy Spirit, Come.

O HOLY Spirit, come.
And Jesus' love declare;
Oh, tell us of our heavenly home,
And guide us safely there.

Come with resistless power,
Come with almighty grace,
Come with the long-expected shower,
And fall upon this place.

Nearer to Thee.

NEARER, my God, to thee!
Nearer to thee.
E'en though it be a cross
That raiseth me,
Still all my song shall be,
Nearer, my God, to thee,
Nearer to thee!

Though like the wanderer,
The sun gone down,
Darkness be over me,
My rest a stone,
Yet in my dreams I'd be,
Nearer, my God, to thee,
Nearer to thee!

There let the way appear,
Steps unto heaven,
All that thou sendest me,
In mercy given,
Angels to beckon me
Nearer, my God, to thee,
Nearer to thee!

Holy Spirit, Faithful Guide.

HOLY Spirit, faithful guide,
Ever near the Christian's side,
Gently lead us by the hand,
Pilgrims in a desert land;
Weary souls fore'er rejoice,
While they hear that sweetest voice
Whispering softly, wanderer come!
Follow me, I'll guide thee home.

Ever-present, truest Friend,
Ever near thine aid to lend,
Leave us not to doubt and fear,
Groping on in darkness drear,
When the storms are raging sore,
Hearts grow faint, and hopes give o'er,—
Whisper softly, wanderer, come!
Follow me, I'll guide thee home!

Coronation.

ALL hail the power of Jesus' name,
Let angels prostrate fall,
Bring forth the royal diadem,
And crown him Lord of all.

Ye chosen seed of Israel's race,
Ye ransomed from the fall,
Hail him who saves you by his grace,
And crown him Lord of all.

Let every kindred, every tribe,
On this terrestrial ball,
To him all majesty ascribe,
And crown him Lord of

O that with yonder sacred throng
We at his feet may fall,
We'll join the everlasting song,
And crown him Lord of all.

Blest be the tie.

BLEST be the tie that binds
Our hearts in Christian love,
The fellowship of kindred minds
Is like to that above.

Before our Father's throne
We pour our ardent prayers;
Our fears, our hopes, our aims are one,
Our comforts and our cares.

We share our mutual woes,
Our mutual burdens bear,
And often for each other flows
The sympathizing tear.

When we asunder part,
It gives us inward pain;
But we shall still be joined in heart,
And hope to meet again.

How Solemn are the Words.

HOW solemn are the words,
And yet to faith how plain,
Which Jesus uttered while on earth,—
"Ye must be born again!"

"Ye must be born again!"
For so hath God decreed,
No reformation will suffice—
Tis LIFE poor sinners need.

"Ye must be born again,!"
And life IN CHRIST must have;
In vain the soul may elsewhere go—
'Tis he ALONE can save.

"Ye must be born again,!"
Or never enter heaven;
'Tis only blood-washed ones are there—
The ransomed are forgiven.

What a Friend.

WHAT a Friend we have in Jesus,
All our sins and griefs to bear,
What a privlege to carry
Everything to God in prayer!
O what peace we often forfeit,
O what needless pain we bear,
All because we do not carry
Everything to God in prayer!

Have we trials and temptations?
Is there trouble anywhere?
We should never be discouraged,
Take it to the Lord in prayer.
Can we find a friend so faithful
Who will all our sorrows share?
Jesus knows our every weakness,
Take it to the Lord in prayer.

Rock of Ages.

ROCK of Ages, cleft for me,
Let me hide myself in thee,
Let the water and the blood,
From thy wounded side which flowed,
Be of sin the double cure,
Save from wrath and make me pure.

Could my tears forever flow,
Could my zeal no languor know,
These for sin could not atone,
Thou must save, and thou alone,
In my hand no price I bring,
Simply to thy cross I cling.

While I draw this fleeting breath,
When my eyes shall close in death,
When I rise to worlds unknown,
And behold thee on thy throne,
Rock of Ages, cleft for me,
Let me hide myself in thee.

Happy Day.

O HAPPY day, that fixed my choice
On thee, my Saviour and my God!
Well may this glowing heart rejoice,
And tell its rapture all abroad.

CHO.—Happy day, happy day,
When Jesus washed my sins away;
He taught me how to watch and pray,
And live rejoicing every day;
Happy day, happy day,
When Jesus washed my sins away.

'Tis done, the great transaction's done—
I am my Lord's and he is mine;
He drew me, and I followed on,
Charmed to confess the voice divine.

Now rest, my long-divided heart,
Fixed on this blissful centre, rest,
Nor ever from thy Lord depart,
With him of every good possessed.

Sweet Hour of Prayer.

prayer,
SWEET hour of prayer, sweet hour of
That calls me from a world of care,
And bids me at my Father's throne
Make all my wants and wishes known!
In seasons of distress and grief
My soul has often found relief,
And oft escaped the tempter's snare
By thy return, sweet hour of prayer.

Sweet hour of prayer, sweet hour of prayer
Thy wings shall my petition bear
To him, whose truth and faithfulness ;
Engage the waiting soul to bless:
And since he bids me seek his face,
Believe his word. and trust his grace,
I'll cast on him my every care,
And wait for thee, sweet hour of prayer.

Work for the night.

WORK for the night is coming,
Work through the morning hours;
Work, while the dew is sparkling,
Work 'mind springing flowers;
Work, when the day grows brighter,
Work in the glowing sun ;
Work, for the night is coming,
When man's work is done.

Work, for the night is coming,
Work through the sunny noon.;
Fill brightest hours with labor,
Rest comes sure and soon.
Give every flying minute
Some.hing to keep in store:
Work, for the night is coming,
When man works no more.

Fountain.

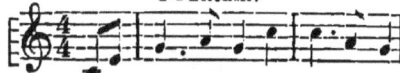

THERE is a fountain filled with blood
Drawn from Immanuel's veins:
And sinners, plunged beneath that flood,
Lose all their guilty stains.

The dying thief rejoiced to see
That fountain in his day:
And there may I, though vile as he,
Wash all my sins away.

Thou dying Lamb! thy precious blood
Shall never lose its power,
Till all the ransomed Church of God
Are saved, to sin no more.

E'er since, by faith, I saw the stream,
Thy flowing wounds supply,
Redeeming love has been my theme,
And shall be till I die,

I Hear Thy Welcome Voice.

I HEAR thy welcome voice,
That calls me, Lord, to thee,
For cleansing in thy precious blood
That flowed on Calvary.

CHO.—I am coming, Lord,:
Coming now to thee !
Wash me, cleanse me in the blood
That flowed on Calvary.

Though coming weak and vile,
Thou dost my strength assure;
Thou dost my vileness fully cleanse,
Till spotless all and pure.

'Tis Jesus calls me on
To perfect faith and love,
To perfect hope, and peace, and trust,
For earth and heaven above.

All hail, atoning blood!
All hail, redeeming grace!
All hail. the gift of Christ our Lord,
Our Strength and Righteousness!

The Home Over There.

OH! think of the home over there,
By the side of the river of light,
Where the saints, all immortal and fair,
Are robed in their garments of white.

REF.—Over there, over there,
Oh, think of the home over there.

Oh. think of the friends over there,
Who before us the journey have trod,
Of the songs that they breathe on the air,
In their home in the palace of God.

REF.—Over there, over there,
Oh, think of the friends over there.

My Saviour is now over there,
There my kindred and friends are at rest;
Then away from my sorrow and care,
Let me fly to the land of the blest.

REF,—Over there, over there,
My Saviour is now over there.

I'll soon be at home over there,
For the end of my journey I see,
Many dear to my heart. over there,
Are watching and waiting for me.

REF.—Over there, over there,
I'll soon be at home over there.

106

Lead Me.

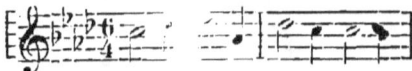

LORD, I hear of showers of blessing
 Thou art scattering full and free—
Showers the thirsty land refreshing,
 Let some droppings fall on me.

Cho.—Even me, even me,
 Let thy blessing fall on me.

Pass me not, O gracious Father!
 Sinful though my heart may be:
Thou might'st leave me, but the rather
 Let thy mercy fall on me.

Pass me not, O tender Saviour!
 Let me love and cling to thee:
I am longing for thy favor:
 Whilst thou'rt calling, oh, call me!

Pass me not, O mighty Spirit!
 Thou canst make the blind to see:
Witnesses of Jesus' merit,
 Speak the word of power to me.

Before the Cross.

MY faith looks up to thee,
 Thou Lamb of Calvary,
 Saviour divine;
Now hear me while I pray,
Take all my guilt away,
O let me from this day
 Be wholly thine.

May thy rich grace impart
Strength to my fainting heart,
 My zeal inspire;
As thou hast died for me,
O may my love to thee
Pure, warm, and changeless be.—
 A living fire.

While life's dark maze I tread,
And griefs around me spread,
 Be thou my guide;
Bid darkness turn to day,
Wipe sorrow's tears away,
Nor let me ever stray
 From thee aside.

Just as I am.

JUST as I am, without one plea,
 But that thy blood was shed for me,
And that thou bid'st me come to thee,
 O Lamb of God, I come!

Just as I am, and waiting not
To rid my soul of one dark blot,
To thee, whose blood can cleanse each spot,
 O Lamb of God, I come!

Just as I am—thou wilt receive,
Wilt welcome, pardon, cleanse, relieve;
Because thy promise I believe,
 O Lamb of God, I come!

Pray for Reapers.

Saints of God! the dawn is brightening,
 Token of our coming Lord;
O'er the earth the field is whitening;
 Louder rings the Master's word:
Pray for reapers
 In the harvest of the Lord.

Feebly now they toil in sadness,
 Weeping o'er the waste around,
Slowly gathering grains of gladness,
 While their echoing cries resound:
Pray that reapers
 In God's harvest may abound.

Now, O Lord! fulfil thy pleasure;
 Breathe upon thy chosen band,
And with Pentecostal measure
 Send forth reapers o'er our land,
Faithful Reapers,
 Gathering sheaves for thy right hand.

Is not this the Land of Beulah?

I am dwelling on the mountain,
 Where the golden sunlight gleams
O'er a land whose wondrous beauty
 Far exceeds my fondest dreams:
Where the air is pure, ethereal,
Laden with the breath of flowers
 That are blooming by the fountain,
 'Neath the amaranthine bowers.

Cho.
Is not this the land of Beulah,
 Blessed, blessed land of light,
Where the flowers bloom forever,
 And the sunlight fadeth not?

I can see far down the mountain,
 Where I wandered weary years,
Often hindered in my journey
 By the ghosts of doubts and fears,
Broken vows and disappointments
 Thickly sprinkled all the way,
But the Spirit led unerring
 To the land I hold to-day.

I am drinking at the fountain,
 Where I ever would abide;
For I've tasted life's pure river,
 And my soul is satisfied;
There's no thirsting for life's pleasures,
 Nor adorning rich and gay,
For I've found a richer treasure,
 One that fadeth not away.

Tell me not of heavy crosses,
 Nor the burdens hard to bear,
For I've found this great salvation
 Makes each burden light appear;
And I love to follow Jesus,
 Gladly counting all but dross,
Worldly honors all forsaking
 For the glory of the Cross.

Marching Home Together.

WILL you join our happy band,
 Marching home together,
Traveling to the better land,
 Marching home together?
Will you wait with us for him
Who will end all sorrow,
Gazing past earth's dark to-day,
To heaven's bright to-morrow?

CHO.—Marching home, marching home,
 Marching home together,
 Heart to heart and hand in hand.
 Marching home together!

Strangers here, we seek no place,
 Marching Home together,
Every step we learn his grace,
 Marching home together,
Every need by him supplied,
 Wakes a note of singing,
Every sorrow sanctified
 Praise to him is bringing.

Every day the miles grow less,
 Marching home together,
As our footsteps onward press,
 Marching home together,
Even now we catch a gleam,
 Hear the chorus swelling,
As each wanderer finds his place
 In the Father's dwelling.

Lord God, the Holy Ghost.

LORD God, the Holy Ghost!
 In this accepted hour,
As on the day of Pentecost,
Descend in all thy power.

Like mighty rushing wind
Upon the waves beneath,
Move with one impulse every mind,
One soul, one feeling breathe.

The young, the old inspire
With wisdom from above,
And give us hearts and tongues of fire,
To pray, and praise, and love.

Spirit of truth! be thou
In life and death our guide·
O Spirit of adoption· now
May we be sanctified.

Have ye Received the Holy Ghost?

Disciples of the Holy One,
 Have ye the Holy Ghost received?
Has heaven's baptismal fire come down
Upon your souls since ye believed?
The great Refiner—has He come
And purified your souls from sin,
And in your hearts set up His home,
And brought his heavenly kingdom in?

The Pentecostal hallowed shower
 Which on the waiting suppliants came,
The blest anointing, sacred power,
 The all-inspiring heavenly flame,
Are all your being's powers imbued
 With Christlike sweetness, holy joy?
With Jesus' blessed mind emdued—
 Do heavenly things your powers employ?

Are you in perfect harmony
 With God's own will each day and hour?
In all things only Him to see,
 And ever feel His saving power?
A spotless soul, a single eye,
 A spirit filled with love and peace;
A life His name to glorify—
 Your God alone to serve and please?

The blessed Comforter divine
 Delights to make us His abode,
In His own brightness thus to shine,
 As trophies of His saving blood.
Oh, Holy Ghost, how blest Thy sway!
 To purify and save each day;
Oh, Christians, have ye yet received
 The Holy Ghost since ye believed?

Tell it to God.

WHATEVER troubles thee,
 Tell it to God;
All thy anxiety,
 Tell it to God;
For every earthly grief
This is thy sweet relief—
 Tell it to God.

That pain which none may know,
 Tell it to God;
That word which grieved thee so,
 Tell it to God;
Earth has no ready cure.
God's sympathy is sure—
 Tell it to God.

Hast thou impatient been?
 Tell it to God;
Art prone through this to sin?
 Tell it to God;
He knows thy weakness all,
Will help thee lest thou fall-
 Tell it to God.

Does care corrode thy life?
 Tell it to God;
Art weary with the strife?
 Tell it to God;
He says, Bring all thy care
To Me, to help thee bear—
 Tell it to God.

Art grieving o'er thy loss?
 Tell it to God;
Art sinking 'neath thy cross?
 Tell it to God;
He can assuage thy pain,
He will with grace sustain—
 Tell it to God.

Whate'er may thee befall,
 Tell it to God;
Thy grief or great or small,
 Tell it to God;
To him bring each request,
In him find joy and rest—
 Tell all to God.

I am Praying for you.

I HAVE a Saviour, he's pleading in glory,
A dear, loving Saviour, tho' earth-friends
be few,
And now he is watching in tenderness o'er
me,
And, oh, that my Saviour, were your Saviour, too!

CHO.—For you I am praying,:‖
I'm praying for you.

I have a Father: to me he has given
A hope for eternity, blessed and true,
And soon will he call me to meet him in
heaven, [me, too!
But, oh, that he'd let me bring you with

I have a robe: 'tis resplendent in whiteness
Awaiting in glory my wondering view;
Oh, when I receive it all shining in brightness,
Dear friend, could I see you receiving one,
too!

What hast thou done for Me?

I GAVE my life for thee,
My precious blood I shed,
That thou might'st ransomed be,
And quickened from the dead;
I gave, I gave My life for thee!
What hast thou given for Me?

My Father's house of light,—
My glory-circled throne,—
I left, for earthly night,
For wand'rings sad and lone:
I left, I left it all for thee!
Hast thou left aught for Me?

I suffered much for thee,
More than thy tongue can tell,
Of bitterest agony.
To rescue thee from hell:
I've borne, I've borne it all for thee.
What hast thou borne for Me?

And I have brought to thee,
Down from my home above,
Salvation full and free,
My pardon and My love;
I bring, I bring rich gifts to thee!
What hast thou brought to Me?

Communion. C. M.

Alas! and did my Saviour bleed?
And did my Sovereign die?
Would He devote that sacred head
For such a worm as I?

Was it for crimes that I have done,
He groaned upon the tree?
Amazing pity! grace unknown!
And love beyond degree!

Well might the sun in darkness hide,
And shut his glories in,
When Christ, the mighty Maker, died
For man, the creature's sin.

Thus might I hide my blushing face
While His dear cross appears:
Dissolve my heart in thankfulness,
And melt mine eyes to tears.

But drops of grief can ne'er repay
The debt of love I owe;
Here, Lord, I give myself away,—
'Tis all that I can do.

Azmon. C. M.

O for a closer walk with God,
A calm and heavenly frame;
A light to shine upon the road
That leads me to the Lamb!

Where is the blessedness I knew
When first I saw the Lord?
Where is the soul-refreshing view
Of Jesus and His word?

What peaceful hours I once enjoyed!
How sweet their memory still!
But they have left an aching void
The world can never fill.

Return, O Holy Dove, return,
Sweet messenger of rest!
I hate the sins that made Thee mourn,
And drove Thee from my breast.

The dearest idol I have known,
Whate'er that idol be,
Help me to tear it from Thy throne,
And worship only Thee.

So shall my walk be close with God;
Calm and serene my frame;
So purer light will mark the road
That leads me to the Lamb.

Naomi. C. M.

Father, whate'er of earthly bliss
Thy sovereign w ll denies,
Accepted at thy throne of grace,
Let this petition rise:

Give me a calm, a thankful heart,
From every murmur free;
The blessings of Thy grace impart
And make me live to Thee.

Let the sweet hope that Thou art mine
My life and death attend;
Thy presence through my journey shine,
And crown my journey's end.

Penitence. 7, 6, 8.

Jesus, let Thy pitying eye
Call back a wandering sheep;
False to Thee, like Peter, I
Would fain, like Peter, weep:
Let me be by grace restored;
On me be all long-suffering shown;
Turn, and look upon me, Lord,
And break my heart of stone.

Saviour, Prince, enthroned above,
Repentance to impart,
Give me, through Thy dying love,
The humble, contrite heart;
Give what I have long implored,
A portion of Thy grief unknown ;
Turn, and look upon me, Lord,
And break my heart of stone.

See me, Saviour, from above,
Nor suffer me to die ;
Life, and happiness, and love
Drop from Thy gracious eye:
Speak the reconciling word,
And let thy mercy melt me down;
Turn, and look upon me, Lord,
And break my heart of stone

The Saints' Home. 11.

'Mid scenes of confusion and creature
complaints,
How sweet to the soul is communion
with saints!
To find at the banquet of mercy there's
room,
And feel in the presence of Jesus at home.
Home ! home ! sweet, sweet home !
Prepare me, dear Saviour, for glory, my
home.

Sweet bonds that unite all the children
of peace !
And, thrice precious Jesus, whose love
cannot cease,
Though oft from Thy presence in sadness
I roam,
I long to behold Thee in glory, at home.

While here in the valley of conflict I
stay,
O give me submission, and strength as
my day;
In all my afflictions to Thee would I
come,
Rejoicing in hope of my glorious home.

Whate'er Thou deniest, O give me Thy
grace,
The Spirit's sure witness, and smiles of
Thy face ;
Endue me w th patience to wait at Thy
throne,
And find even now, a sweet foretaste of
home.

Mount Pisgah. C. M.

On Jordan's stormy banks I stand,
And cast a wishful eye
To Canaan's fair and happy land,
Where my possessions lie.

O the transporting, rapturous scene,
That rises to my sight !
Sweet fields arrayed in living green,
And rivers of delight.

Over all those wide-extended plains
Shines one eternal day;
There God, the Son, forever reigns,
And scatters night away.

No chilling winds or poisonous breath
Can reach that healthful shore.
Sickness and sorrow, pain and death,
Are felt, and feared, no more.

When shall I reach that happy place,
And be forever blest?
When shall I see my Father's face,
And in His bosom rest ?

Filled with delight, my raptured soul
Would here no longer stay;
Though Jordan's waves around me roll,
Fearless I'd launch away.

5

FOREST.

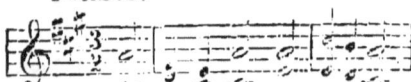

MY soul ! what hast thou done for God ?
  Look o'er thy misspent years and see;
Sum up what thou hast done for God,
  And then what God has done for thee.

He made thee when he might have made
  A soul that would have loved him   more;
He rescued thee from nothingness.
  And set thee on life's happy shore.

He placed an angel at thy side,
  And strewed joys round thee on thy way;
He gave thee rights thou couldst not claim,
  And life, free life, before thee lay.

What hast thou done for God, my soul ?
  Look o'er thy misspent years and see;
Cry from thy worse than nothingness,
  Cry for his mercy upon thee !

VARINA.

I carried many a weary load
  In prayer to God each day;
Much though upon my cares bestowed,
  Then through my load away.
I let it bear my spirits down
  With an oppressive weight;
I asked the Lord my faith to crown,
  But would not trust to wait.

I feared to let my burdens lie
  Upon the altar there,
But watched them with a jealous eye,
  And named them oft in prayer.
But never would I trust the Lord,
  And leave them in his hand;
I could not grasp His faithful word,
  Or follow His command.

Till he refused to let me take
  The gift I one day brought;
For I had said; "For Jesus sake,"
  Thy will in me be wrought.
Then with new light He filled my soul,
  And I was truly blest;
My cares were under his control,
  My weary soul found rest.

ELTESME.

IN this hour of consecration,
  Lord, I give myself to thee:
Breathe the quickening Holy Spirit;
  Let it fall and rest on me,
Change and purify my nature;
  Fill me with thy peace divine,
Wash me in the blood of cleansing,
  Seal me thine, forever thine.

Laid upon thine holy altar.
  Take the gift for Jesus' sake:
'Tis but my weak heart I bring thee,
  A poor sacrifice to make;
This I bring, with tears and trembling;
  O how poor my gift and small !
But, dear Father, do not spurn it;
  Bringing this, I bring my all.

O how oft, before thee bended,
  I have struggled with my will !
And but for thy Holy Spirit,
  It would be unconquered still,
Heavenly Father, take my offering.
  Lest my heart and courage fail;
Breathe on me the quickening Spirit ?
  Let my prayer with thee prevail.

GREENVILLE.

BEAR me out, O blessed Jesus !
  Let me get beyond this shore,
Bear me out in deeper water,
  Where I'll find my "self" no more;
Filled with all thy fullness, Jesus,
  Lost in that unbounded sea,
Without effort calmly floating,
  Previously upborne by thee.

Let the tide of full salvation
  Higher rise within my soul,
'Till my beings ransomed powers
  Own thy sweet and full control;
'Till I know thy love's completeness,
  'Till it floods this heart of mine;
'Till I'm filled with all the fullness,
  Sealed and sanctified as thine.

Bear me out, O blessed Jesus !
  On thy love's unbounded sea,
Drifting on its depths unfathome
  To the great eternity,
There to see thy full perfection,
  To behold thy form divine,
And with all the saved and blood-
    washed
Radiant in thy courts to shine.

ALETTA.

LORD, I want to feel thy power
  In this precious, precious, hour,
Give to me thy grace divine,
  As with fire my soul refine.

O for more of holy power !
  Lord, in this auspicious hour,
Seal me with thy grace divine;
  As with fire my soul refine.

Work in me the death to sin;
  Even now the work begin;
Let thy grace, revealed in me,
  Bind me more and more to thee.

May thy soul-transforming love
  Come, this moment, from above,
Into this weak heart of mine,
  Its affections to refine.

The Sinner and the Saviour.

Tune, page 28.

I have no riches of my own,
But Thou, dear Lord, hast bought me,
I was a wanderer far from Thee.
But Thou hast loved and sought me,
This sou to Christ, which thou hast bought,
I now thee surrender;
This heart which thou hast loved and sought,
Through love is waxing tender.

I have no righteousness in me,
My goodness unavailing·
But, Jesu Thine is what I want,
For it is prevailing.
That righteousness encircles me.
And when to o'er sin I'm grieving,
I look from out my soul at Thee,
And seeing is believing.

I know that Thou wilt not forsake,
A child whom Thou dost cherish;
The frail her creature, trusting Thee,
Was never left to perish,
Lord, hold me fast, and from Thy side,
Nor time. nor death can sever;
Thine here below—a ransomed life—
And Thine above forever.

C. M.

Jesus, thine all-victorious love
Shed in my heart abroad;
Then shall my feet no longer rove,
Rooted and fix'd in God.

O that in me the sacred fire
Might now begin to glow:
Burn up the dross of base desire,
And make the mountains flow.

O that it now from heaven might fall,
And all my sins consume;
Come, Holy Ghost, for thee I call;
Spirit of burning, come,

Refining fire, go through my heart;
Illuminate my soul:
Scatter thy life through every part,
And sanctify the whole

My steadfast soul, from falling free,
Shall then no longer move;
While Christ is all the world to me,
And all my heart is love.

C. M.

Enthroned on high, Almighty Lord,
The Holy Ghost send down:
Fulfil in us thy faithful word,
And all thy mercies crown,

Though on our heads no tongues of fire
Their wondrous powers impart,
Grant, Saviour, what we most desire,—
Thy Spirit in our heart,

To our benighted minds reveal
The glories of his grace,
And bring us where no clouds conceal,
The brightness of his face.

His love within us shed abroad,—
Life's ever-springing well;
Till God in us, and we in God,
In love eternal dwell

L. M.

Take up thy cross, the saviour said,
If thou wouldst My disciple be;
Deny thyself, the world forsake,
And humbly follow after Me.

Take up thy cross; let not its weight
Fill thy weak spirit with alarm,
His strength shall bear thy spirit up,
And brace thy heart, and nerve thine arm.

Take up thy cross, nor heed the shame
Nor let thy foolish pride rebel:
Thy Lord for thee the Cross endured,
To save thy soul from death and hell,

Take up thy cross then in His strength,
And calmly every danger brave;
'Twill guide thee to a better home,
And lead to victory o'er the grave.

Take up thy cross, and follow Christ,
Nor think till death to lay it down;
For only he who bears thy cross,
May hope to wear the glorious crown.

Tune Greenville.

Come, then all-inspiring Spirit,
Into every longing heart!
Bought for us by Jesus' merit,
Now thy blissful self impart.

CHO:—Keep us from the world unspotted,
From all earthly passions free,
Wholly to thyself devoted,
Fixed to live and die for thee.

Sign our uncontested pardon;
Wash us in atoning blood;
Make our hearts a watered garden;
Fill our thirsty souls with God.

Claim us for thy habitation;
Dwell within our hallowed breast;
Seal us heirs of full salvation,
Fitted for our heavenly rest.

Peace, the seal of sin forgiven,
Joy, and perfect love impart,
Press in, everlasting heaven,
All thou hast and all thou art.

INDEX.

A Harp, a Robe, A Crown 83
All hail the power of Jesus name......104
Awake, O heavenly Wind 66
Azmon ... ., ...118

Bear me out, O blessed Jesus.............110
Be not faithless.... 72
Be thou my help 79
Blest be the tie that binds 104
Bringing in the sheaves 7
Brother, pray for my soul 36

Calvary 21
Closer to thee. 52
Come, Holy Spirit 90
Come to Him 49
Come, trust, pray 64
Communion.........................108

Disciples of the Holy One.............107
Don't forget to pray 80
Don't keep Jesus waiting.............. 43
Do you know the wondrous story.......... 71

Each day a little nearer..................... 82

Faith Hymn.—Trusting Jesus 40
Father, lead me.................. 74
Fill me now 97
For you and for me...................... 89

Gathering Home 99
Go work in my vineyard 84
Grace! 'tis a charming sound............102

Hallelujah! what a Savior 91
Hark! a thrilling voice is sounding ... 93
Have more faith in Jesus 19
Have you heard the news 94
He knows best 57
Holy Spirit, faithful guide 103
Holy Spirit, pity me 34
How sweet the name of Jesus sounds ... 103

I am coming... 50
I am dwelling on the mountain......106
I am praying for you....................108
I am sweetly saved in Jesus 88
I am the Lord's forever 53
I am with thee every hour............. 87
I carried many a weary load.............110
I hear thy welcome voice ... .105
I love thy kingdom, Lord.............105
I need thee, Lord 23
In Heaven w'll meet againe...............101
In the cross of Christ I glory............ 85
In the Life Boat................... 14
In the shadow of the cross................ 67
In the shadow of the Rock............. 20
In this hour of consecration..............110
It is brighter over there.................... 42
I've found a friend........................ 28
I want to be a worker..................... 38

Jesus is able to save...................... 56
Jesus is calling for thee.................. 1
Jesus lover of my soul..................... 63
Jesus now is passing by.................. 54
Jesus said it would be so.................. 65
Jesus, saves me now..................... 82
Jesus shall have it all 59
Jesus will give you rest.................... 96
Just as I am, without one plea............106

Lord God, the Holy Ghost.............107
Lord, I hear of showers of blessing......106
Lord, I want to feel thy power.............110

Make me a worker for Jesus 12
My beautiful home above.............. 48
Mt. Pisgah...........................108
My faith looks up to thee............106
My sacrifice..... 93
My soul, what hast thou done for God?...110

Naomi . .. .109
Nearer Home 70
Nearer, my God, to thee.................103
Not for from the kingdom 98
Now my heart is full of rapture 75

O Happy day that fixed my choice......104
O Holy Spirit, come ... .103
Oh, think of the home over there 105
O mourner in Zion, how blessed art thou.102
O ye who seek the Saviour 102
Only in the name of Jesus.... 25
Only near to the kingdom 6
Only remembered by what I have done... 61
Our dear happy home 58

Penitence.. 109
Precious blood of Jesus 92

Rest, sweet rest 29
Rock of Ages (Bass Solo)............. 62
Rock of Ages, cleft for me................104

Sacred season of Communion............ 4
Saints of God, the dawn is brightening.106
Satisfied by and by...................... 26
Saved 8
Save the Boy 13
Seeking Peace and Rest.................. 60
Soft and low 51
Soldier's of Zion 9
Sometime, somewhere... 37
Standing on the mighty Rock. 15
Sweet hour of Prayer.................105
Sweet Paradise 68

Tell us something more 60
The child of a King 5
The Fountain 92
The Golden Light 24
The half has never been told.... 10
The hand to which I cling.............. 22
The Holy Ghost is come.................102
The land is drawing near............. 81
The quite vale prayer................... 2
There is a fountain filled with blood.....105
The saints home 109
The three fold promise 46
The very best for Jesus.................. 18
The warm, warm heart of Jesus........ 35
Too late—no room.... 95

Vale of Beulah.......................... 33
Vaughn 96

Waiting at the cross.................... 31
Wandering sinner, return.............. 39
Washed and cleansed... 86
Wash me in the blood of the Lamb....... 94
We'll be there......................... 41
We meet now in thy name... 102
We pray for thy blessing ,............. 44
We shall rest in the cool of the day......100
What a friend we have in Jesus.......... 104
Whatever troubles thee.................107
What hast thou done for me 108
What will you do in that day?........... 77
Who will be there? 27
Whosoever believeth 78
Whosoever will, let him come and be sav'd 45
Why not come to him now?............. 47
Why not trust in him now?....;........ 11
Will you and I be there? 55
Will you be washed in the blood?......... 16
Will you come to the cross?............. 20
Will you join our happy band?............107
Wonderful grace....................... 73
Wonderful love....................... 17
Work, for the night is coming.......... 105
Would you meet me in the kingdom...... 76

•

SPIRITUAL SONGS.

WHAT PEOPLE THINK OF IT,

"Spiritual Songs" seems to please our school so much that we have decided to order—— copies more.

J. D. KEYES, Mount Vision, N. Y. Feb. 21st, 1881.

We have needed something of the kind a long time; have been looking for it, and feel we have found it.

G. H. PATTILLO, Milledgeville, Ga. Feb. 21st, 1881.

Your books go like "hot cakes."

REV. JAMES WALES, Elkhart, Ind. March 10th, 1881.

Our boys pronounce it a "Jewel."

GEO. H. RICHTER, Pres. Y. M. C. A., Lowville, N. Y. March 7th, 1881.

I consider "Spiritual Songs" unequaled by any collection I have yet seen.

C. A. STEFFEY, Royal Center, Ind. March 7th, 1881.

The general expression is, "I don't see how they can afford so much real worth for so small pay."

DANIEL N. CLINE, Conklin Forks, N. Y. Feb. 24th, 1881.

G. W. Rease, Conductor of S. S. Music, M. E. S. S., South Whitley, Ind. We think it is the only book published that should take the place of Gospel Hymns and Sacred Songs.

Rev. E. S. Lorenz, Dayton, Ohio. The best of all your good books.

The "Advance," Chicago, Ill. A good thing, a very good thing, about the new Sunday School Hymn book by Rev. E. A. Hoffman and J. H. Tenney, called "Spiritual Songs for Gospel meetings," is the inclusion of some two hundred of the most familiar hymns and spiritual songs, old and new. These make a choice and rich selection of great convenience and value.

The "Evangelical Messenger," Cleveland. The production of two well known authors, with whose work the singing public has already become familiar by their former successful books as well as by their contributions to almost every music book lately issued from the press. Rev. Elisha A. Hoffman has become familiar with the wants of the people by his experience in pastoral work and in holding Gospel Meetings, and in training Sunday Schools, etc., in song, and the book is adapted to meet these wants. The Hymns are excellent, spiritual in tone, and well express the various states of the soul. They are wedded to good music, devotional and singable.

The National Baptist, Philadelphia. The examination of this book has given us genuine satisfaction. We find both the hymns and tunes admirably fitted for devotional purpose. The simple names of both editors are a guarantee for superior achievement in this department of holy worship.

The "Banner of Zion," Knoxville, O. We consider it a masterpiece in the song book line—the best we have seen, lately. It contains a fine selection of new music never before printed, and other pieces now very popular.

The "National Sunday School Teacher,"—Chicago. The tunes are of the sort that take hold, and the words much better than the average. In it are some half dozen pieces by Bliss hitherto unpublished. Give the book an examination.

The "Christian Standard and Home Journal," Philadelphia, Pa. Contains a good number of pieces of music of great excellence.

The "Methodist," New York. Contains excellent hymns which number over two hundred—the music is rich. The value of the book is worth more than its price of 25 cents for a single copy, or $20 per 100.

The "Christian Advocate," Nashville, Tenn. This is rather above the average work of the kind. Good poetry and sweet music are both to be found therein, and we can recommend it to Sunday Schools.

The "Central Christian Advocate," St. Louis. The authors of this volume are well known and have had experience in holding meetings and training schools. We find many favorite hymns in these pages.

The "Religious Telescope," Dayton, O. It will be found to possess real merit. A very appropriate and desirable feature is the twenty-seven pages containing the best standard old hymns from the regular collections. These with the fresh and appropriate music of the book, make it one of the best we have yet seen for religious meetings.

The "Morning Star," Dover N. H. It is prepared by Rev. Elisha A. Hoffman and J. H. Tenney, both of whom have something of a reputation of musical authors. The volume contains some really excellent pieces, and will be likely to receive a fair share of public favor.

The "Living Epistle," Cleveland, O. A good selection of such popular revival songs as the people are bound to sing.

The Christian Harvester," Cleveland, O. The best book since Winnowed Hymns.

"Zion's Herald," Boston, Mass. Its hymns seem to have been selected with more than usual care.

The Northern "Christian Advocate," Syracuse, N. Y. Uniform in size with the Gospel Song series and very similar in character. The name of P. P. Bliss as a contributor, appears quite frequently in the collection. There are many new pieces and new authors.